Borderland Christianity

Borderland Christianity

Critical Reason and the Christian Vision of Love

James W. Woelfel

Nashville   Abingdon Press   New York

BORDERLAND CHRISTIANITY
Copyright © 1973 by Abingdon Press

Library of Congress Cataloging in Publication Data

Woelfel, James W. Borderland Christianity. Includes
bibliographical references. 1. Christianity—Philosophy.
I. Title.

BR100.W6   201'.1   73-4004
ISBN 0-687-03849-9

MANUFACTURED BY THE PARTHENON PRESS AT
NASHVILLE, TENNESSEE, UNITED STATES OF AMERICA

To Judy

And for all this, nature is never spent;
There lives the dearest freshness deep down things . . .

Gerard Manley Hopkins
"God's Grandeur"

Acknowledgments

In my research and writing I think of myself as a "loner," relying much more on books and individual reflection than on dialogue with colleagues and students. I recognize the large temperamental element in this closeted approach to scholarship, together with its advantages and its disadvantages. But as I look back over the long and erratic course which led to this book, I am gratified to be able to recall a number of others who in small and large ways have helped it along the way.

I could not have devoted summers to hacking away in my characteristically amorphous and ever-changing manner at bits and pieces of what follows, without grants in 1968, 1969, and 1970 from the General Research Fund of the University of Kansas. I wish to express my appreciation to the individuals and committees all the way up the line for their confidence in a project the ending of which barely resembles its beginning. In this connection, a special word of thanks goes to Professor Richard DeGeorge, former chairman of the Philosophy Department, for his tireless support and help on more occasions than I probably even realize.

I am grateful, too, for a sabbatical leave from the University during the academic year 1972-73, which gave me (among other things) the needed leisure to give revisions and other details of preparation for publication the attention they deserved. My thanks go also to the Philosophy Department of the University, in the persons of its chairman Professor Rex Martin and its former secretary Mrs. Ruth Ann Rooney, for finding the funds and making the arrangements to have the manuscript typed in its final form. Miss Patricia Quinn, a student in the University's work-study program, did the typing, often from rough drafts which were almost illegibly so, with gratefully received results.

Less tangible but not less appreciated were ideas and problems I picked up or had clarified in conversations and discussions with colleagues and students in the Philosophy Department and the School of Religion. These often took hold so imperceptibly and latently at the time, and became so integrated into the rest of my thinking, that it would be impossible to pinpoint specific persons or contributions. Such fruitful and enjoyable interchanges constitute an important qualification of my basically introspective approach to research and writing. I think back, too, with gratitude and a bit of a wince to the groups of lay people, clergymen, and religion scholars who at various times earnestly suffered my first enthusiastic but fumbling attempts to formulate my "ecstatic humanism" perspective.

Two of the essays that follow, "The Logic of Ultimate Hope" and "The Resurrection: Between Scylla and Charybdis" (both now revised), appeared in *The Christian Century* and elicited some published and personal responses which I appreciated. The chapter on Albert Schweitzer and the historical Jesus began and almost ended its life long ago and in quite different form as a graduate school essay and a failed article manuscript. The criticisms on both occasions were most helpful, and were incorporated into its metamorphosis. Although they would hardly recognize it now, my philosophy colleagues read and discussed a brief and barely germinated form of "The Dilemma of Omnipotent Love" as a colloquium paper a few years ago, when I still believed that the divine omnipotence was defensible but was greatly troubled by it. They were also "treated" to some of my problems with the historical Jesus and the uses theologians make of him, in a more recent colloquium paper, the spirit, if not the matter, of which survives in the present book. My religion colleague and good friend Professor John Macauley, who has helped me in so many ways through our years together, kindly read the essay on the resurrection shortly after it was first written and made a few suggestions which I have incorporated.

The reader will notice throughout the book several enthusiastic references to Father Gregory Baum's book, *Man Becoming*. It was my privilege and pleasure to get acquainted with Father Baum when he came to the University of Kansas in August of 1971 as one of the leaders of a Consultation on Styles of Theological Reflection for the Future sponsored by the School of Religion and the United Ministries in Higher Education. Preparation for the Consultation was the occasion for my reading *Man Becoming*, which I regard as one of the most exciting and creative theological explorations I have seen in years as well as one of the few books that make living sense out of Christianity for me. Father Buam in person fleshed out the perspective of his book in a charming and stimulating way throughout what turned out to be a truly memorable consultation. I acknowledge with gratitude his help with some of my own theological concerns, while dissociating him in advance from all the things in this book with which I am fairly sure he would disagree. If I could, I would also express my appreciation to America's timeliest philosopher, William James, but he departed this mortal frame some sixty-three years ago now. His enduring contribution is an eager openness and sensitivity to the multi-dimensionality of human experience and of reality itself. That side of my own thought which has searched for an empirical outlook that does not flatten and reduce reality met in James an older and wiser companion of incomparable "style."

Typically but very sincerely, I wish in conclusion to thank my wife, Judith Dutton Woelfel, for her intimate companionship in our common religious quest. It is she more than anyone else to whom I pour out my religious doubts and difficulties and whatever positive insights I come up with from day to day. It is she more than anyone else who is a kindred spirit to me, responding with keen interest, questionings, and good suggestions of her own as we find our way together. This book talks about a number of things Judy and I have often discussed and continue to discuss, and to her it is appropriately and gratefully dedicated.

J. W. W.

Contents

Introduction:
Ecstatic Humanism with Christian Hopes

For several years now I have lived and worked, to use Paul Tillich's famous self-description, "on the boundary" between theism (chiefly Christianity) and humanism. Two basic, often conflicting elements have characterized my ongoing search for truth: On the one hand there has been a "natural religiousness," which has always been filled with wonder over the mysteries of existence and has found it extremely difficult to dismiss some of the central things religion experiences and talks about as purely illusory. On the other hand I have possessed a "natural skepticism" which has had a strong taste for facts, for publicly adjudicable realities, and has been ceaselessly suspicious and critical of many religious claims. The juxtaposition of the two has created numerous and endlessly varied inner tensions and conflicts, both intellectual and personal, throughout the years of my education, teaching, and research in the fields of theology and philosophy.

Sometimes I find myself in the position of what the British philosopher Ronald Hepburn once aptly described as a "sceptic with a naturally religious mind" [1]—a kind of open-minded, "reverent" humanist. At other times I think of myself as a kind of ultra-liberal "Christian heretic." I enter with equal gusto and sympathetic interest into the world view of Albert Camus and a discussion of Jesus' resurrection. I teach jointly in two departments of the university, philosophy and religion. Most of my colleagues in philosophy are humanists and skeptics about religion. They are interested in a number of things besides religion, and help keep me healthily absorbed in other issues and areas of knowledge. My colleagues in religion are an ecumenical bunch of theists—active Christians and Jews—with whom I feel completely comfortable both intellectually and personally.

Strangely enough, perhaps, I do not feel schizophrenic about all this. I do have a position, an orientation—albeit a very broad and open-ended one—which I describe below and which comes out more indirectly in the essays that follow. But it is precisely an orientation which straddles the boundary between humanism and religious belief. From my vantage point in the borderlands between largely Christian theism and humanism I make exploratory and critical forays, now into theological and now into secular territory. My situation, I believe, bestows a certain dual perspective and freedom from special pleading which are perhaps of value in engendering some insights of a particular sort into both territories. The essays in this book represent my recent excursions on the theological side which express some long-standing concerns of mine.

A "fence-straddling" perspective such as mine is by

14

no means unique or even unusual these days. The past fifteen years or so of theological ferment have been marked perhaps above all by an increasingly warm appreciation of the secular sphere among theologians. The prison writings of the young German theologian Dietrich Bonhoeffer, who was executed by the Nazis in 1945 for his participation in the resistance plot to assassinate Hitler, have probably functioned as the chief pioneer and symbol of this secular interest.[2] In recent years some well-known younger American theologians have moved steadily away from "neo-orthodox" Christian theology and into broadly humanistic positions which retain a central preoccupation with religious issues. I have in mind such thinkers as the "death of God" theologian William Hamilton, Paul van Buren of *The Secular Meaning of the Gospel* fame, and Sam Keen, formerly a seminary professor and now a consulting editor of *Psychology Today*.[3] In general, a blurring of the boundaries in varying degrees between Christianity and humanism is a fact of contemporary theological life. The problems I raise for Christian theology in the essays comprising this book arise from the sorts of concerns which are important to humanists; the possibilities I suggest for Christianity spring from my continuing close sympathies with the Christian enterprise.

But to explain at somewhat more length where I find myself at the present time: My natural religiousness has at certain periods sought to stifle the sometimes unbearable pain of skepticism by embracing some well-defined religious certainty. My chief temptations have been Roman Catholicism or some rigorous form of confessional Protestantism. Such has been a not uncommon type of convert to Catholicism. A close college friend, now a Catholic priest after a rather different sort of religious quest from mine, used to tell me that if you scratch a Roman Catholic convert you are as likely as not to find a deep-seated skeptic. The leap into religious certainty is the perpetual temptation of the uneasy skeptic. But the religious certitudes I have grasped at from time to time were always unstable in my hands and sooner or later constituted for me a betrayal of my mind—and, since according to Christianity the mind has its source in the wisdom of God, I could not see how God could blame me for honestly using it, even if it led me away from what was perhaps his "true revelation."

At other times the naturally skeptical in me has overcome the naturally religious, and I have flirted with a hard-nosed, purely secular humanism from which the possibility of ultimate meaning and value, of transcendent reality and the transcendence of human spirit and its destiny, is excluded. Perhaps the existentialist philosophies of Jean-Paul Sartre and Albert Camus have been the most tempting to me here (despite their philosophical problems), although I have also been attracted by the "scientific humanism" more characteristic of British and American philosophy and prominently represented by a thinker like John Dewey.

But in the last analysis I have found both extremes —a confident religious certitude and a purely secular humanism—unacceptable. Historical knowledge of the various religions and philosophical knowledge of their ideas have made all of them too problematic for me to espouse any one as the "true faith," although I am continually learning from some of their insights and am awed by the experience and lives of some of their saints and prophets. All this definitely applies to Christianity, and to it in a decisive sense. For Christianity is the religion which has decisively shaped and permeated our Western culture and dominates the world of religion by sheer numbers and influence; it is the religion in whose origins, history, and ideas the American or European religious thinker is ordinarily the most well-versed; it is the religion in which almost all of us in the United States or Europe were nurtured and in terms of which our religious difficulties and possibilities are most likely to be conceived. It is therefore Christianity with which most religiously perplexed people must come to grips in a special way, since it has both created our problems and will probably offer the most natural resources for our groping solutions. What I have to say in the rest of this book reflects this special and personal relationship to Christianity in terms of both its problems and its possibilities.

The person such as myself who wants to build his "philosophy of life" or world view upon public knowledge and experience insofar as possible must be content religiously with uncertainties, with possibilities, with tentativeness and openness in the face of the great deal we do not know about the mysteries of our own existence and of the universe around us. The person whom modern scientific knowledge and methods of investigation have encouraged to be attentive to actual experience in a disciplined manner is obliged, it seems to me, to be "reverently agnostic" about a number of religious claims. To be sure, I would want to argue that this very attentiveness to actual human experience provides ample and insistent grounds for an affirmatively open-minded attitude on such matters as, for example, religious experience and psychic phenomena which only an *un*-scientific, truncated secularism can ignore or disallow. But nothing we can get at in this way of some of the things which religion talks about is at this stage of our knowledge more than not wildly implausible hypotheses or "possibilities"—rich possibilities, to be sure, which keep me humble, open, and full of wonder about existence; but nothing I can invest in with the certainty, the confidence, the detailed elaboration which characterize most religious belief.

My natural skepticism has tempered my natural religiousness in the manner I have described. It has led me increasingly to derive my knowledge from purely human and public sources—largely the natural and social sciences—which are based upon disciplined examination of our experience and seek the most adequate theories to explain and predict that experience. I have just as importantly gleaned rich insights into personal and social human life from literature, the arts, and the religions, which must be included in any full and sensitive account of our human existence and very crucially reveal the always tentative and less-than-whole character of purely scientific theories about and methods of investigating man. But in dealing with all these data of human experience I am guided by purely human criteria of investigation and knowledge, above all by the canons of careful reasoning. Naturally I cannot exempt the religious traditions from this humanistic, experiential approach to knowledge. On the one hand this has produced in me a critical, cautious, relativistic assessment of the religions. On the other hand, this same reliance on human experience and its disciplined investigation has opened up the religious dimension for me in a new way. Thus a hard-headed demand for actual experience, for "the facts," has led me simultaneously into radical criticism of the religions and reverent openness to possible dimensions of reality to which they inadequately try to point.

If the religious extreme of adherence to the certainties of a particular faith has been unacceptable to me, no less so has been the skeptical extreme of a purely secular humanism. A humanist I definitely consider myself, as I will discuss in a moment; but a completely secular humanism, which in various ways closes itself off arbitrarily from religion and the possibility of transcendence, I regard as intellectually truncated and inconsistent. I have toyed, in moments of supreme personal confidence about life and knowledge, with purely secular humanisms, only to find them irrationally narrow and self-confident. When secular humanisms, for example, confidently deny the reality of the divine, declare religion to be completely illusory, and explain away the human spirit in biological or behavioral terms, they then cease to be genuinely skeptical and scientific and are simply dogmatic—thereby emulating one of the chief sins of the religious outlooks which they have rejected.

Modern liberal humanism, which has grown out of the Enlightenment of the eighteenth century, is one of the noblest movements in the history of mankind, and I think of myself as a member of that tradition. Much that is good in contemporary European and American culture is the product of humanist thought and activity during the past two hundred years. The humanistic outlook has been marked by a central dedication to man (hence the name "humanism")—to the growth of humane and scientific knowledge and its application to the rational solution of human problems, the alleviation of human oppression and suffering, the enlargement of individual human rights and freedoms, the widening of educational, social, cultural, and economic opportunities —in general, to the enhancement of the quality of human life. The humanist tries to base his life and his decisions upon the best knowledge he has of man and the world, especially through the sciences, and to seek thoughtful, reasoned solutions to human problems. He looks to human criteria in his thinking and living, because he believes that this is all we have to go on in any solid and public way. The humanist may have religious aspirations and hopes, a reverent sense of the mystery and wonder of existence, or he may not; but if he has, he believes that he must proceed cautiously and tentatively in this elusive area.

All this I hold as a liberal humanist. What I must criticize is what I have called "purely secular" forms of humanism: i.e., explicitly atheistic or reductionistic versions of humanism. My criticism is not directed at their total reliance upon human criteria of knowledge and value, which I share. Nor is it intended to vitiate most of the specific contents of what the purely secular humanist has to say. Since we share the same human standards in the matter of knowledge and value, various humanistic findings are subject to the ordinary sorts of assessment and criticism which derive from reason and observation. On a large number of issues there is no need to raise the kinds of fundamental criticism of atheistic or reductionistic forms of humanism which I am raising here, and all humanists learn much from and rely upon one another's insights.

But it is precisely some of the most vitally important issues—those pertaining to the study and evaluation of our human experience itself—which demand vigorous dissent from the conclusions of purely secular humanism. This has to be done, not in the name of religious belief or of some other trans-humanistic consideration, but in the name of humanism itself. Atheistic and reductionistic humanisms must be seen as inadequate, truncated humanisms. They are not fully humanistic because they are not open to all that man and his encompassing universe possibly are. They are not sufficiently sensitive either to the range and depth of the human spirit or to the limitations of our situation and knowledge. They tend arbitrarily to draw boundaries around human experience and the world and presumptuously to declare that the matter is closed, the reality completely described and circumscribed. This is simply insensitivity to data, to "the facts," and overconfident reasoning—both of which are aberrations of the humanist approach to knowledge.

I hasten to add that there are varieties and degrees of what I have called "purely secular" humanism. The atheism of Albert Camus is not the atheism of Jean-Paul Sartre. Sartre's atheism is confident, impatient, narrow.[4] The atheism of Camus is that of a man who wants heroically to live only with what he knows for sure. It is an atheism with a profound grasp of the religious consciousness and particularly the Christian tradition (at least in its Catholic form), an atheism which translates the language of grace and benediction into the world of the human and the natural. Camus denies the Christian God more because he believes him to be unjust than because he is improbable; the heavens are filled not so much with nothingness as with silence.[5] Nor can the reductionistic scientific humanism of Julian Huxley be lumped indiscriminately with that of Bertrand Russell. Russell tended to be peremptory and hostile about religion in general and Christianity in particular.[6] Huxley, on the other hand, has been one of those "instinctively religious" persons who has gone extensively into the literature of religion and in numerous writings advanced with almost evangelistic fervor his own religion of "evolutionary humanism," transmuting traditional doctrines and religious experience into new, completely this-worldly forms for modern science-dominated man.[7] I have chosen simply a few prominent examples of atheistic and reductionistic humanists to point out that there are degrees of sensitivity, openness, and wonder even within "purely secular" humanism. What all share, however, is an intellectually arbitrary refusal to consider human experience in its fullness, with the various religious possibilities which that includes, and in most cases also an insufficient appreciation of the implications of our finite situation and its limited knowledge.

A truly whole and adequate humanism is one which, precisely in its absorbing preoccupation with man, is sensitively open to the possibility that man himself may be more than we think at any given time—that he may, for example, be a creature involved with dimensions of reality of which our knowledge either is ignorant or has only scratched the surface. Very importantly, these possibilities can in turn enlarge our picture of what we are as human beings. If, for example, the human spirit is in touch with, and opens out onto, an aspect of reality which interacts with, but transcends, spatio-temporal phenomena; if the human personality survives death in some way—if these are possibilities which must be entertained by a humanism which desires to be whole, open-ended, and sensitive to *all* the data of human experience, then such possibilities have decided implications for our knowledge of man, including such things as the relationship between mind and body and the phenomenon of man's religions.

I believe that my "natural religiousness," expanded and reinforced by my broad training in the humanities (philosophy, theology, history, classical and modern literature), has prevented my "natural skepticism" from finding security or satisfaction in purely secular forms of humanism. My skeptical inclinations have forbidden my grasping onto the dogmatic certainties of a particular religious faith for any length of time; my instinctive wonder and openness about the mysteries of our human existence have kept me away from the dogmatic certainties of most atheistic and reductionistic forms of humanism. Of course, the influence of these two basic elements in my makeup has not been as neatly separated and allocated as my remarks may seem to suggest. The very character of my natural religiousness, with its interest in, and fascination with, the universal in man's religious experience, has helped to call me back repeatedly from religious particularity and certainty. Similarly, it has been my very skepticism which has also contributed to a suspicious and critical view of purely secular humanisms, which are very skeptical about some things but curiously unskeptical and overconfident about others.

I would describe the perspective to which I have come (and in which I hope I am always growing and remaining open) as an *"ecstatic" or "self-transcending" humanism*. The Greek word *ek-stasis* literally means "standing outside of." We are familiar with the ordinary usage of "ecstasy" to describe certain psychological and physical states in which a person seems to be "standing outside" himself, to transcend his ordinary self. Most of us have probably experienced ecstasy in sexual love, or perhaps when totally caught up in listening to certain kinds of music; and we have at least heard about phenomena such as whirling dervishes, trances of various sorts, and mystical states.

Following the lead of philosophers such as Paul Tillich, however, I am not using the word "ecstatic" in its ordinary sense; instead I am applying its etymological suggestions of "transcending" or "going beyond" to something much broader. In my case, "ecstatic" is an apt description of the kind of humanistic outlook I wish to commend. "Ecstatic" humanism is a humanistic perspective which *transcends* or *goes beyond* purely secular forms of humanism. Ecstatic humanism is humanism which, precisely because of its preoccupation with human experience in its fullness, seeks to be sensitively open-minded about the possibility of dimensions of experience and reality beyond our present knowing. Ecstatic humanism tries to remain constantly aware of the limitations of the human situation and human knowledge. Ecstatic humanism makes positive contact with, and learns much from, the religious traditions while remaining "reverently agnostic" about many of their details. Ecstatic humanism is too filled with wonder over the mysteries surrounding our existence to be content with narrow, reduced accounts of man and his world.

In its attitude of wonder, openness, religiousness, ecstatic humanism also transcends or goes beyond purely secular humanisms in a sense somewhat akin to the ordinary usage of "ecstatic." Ecstatic humanism is likely to be personally attuned to those aspects of human experience which singularly "take us out of ourselves" —religious experience, love, art and beauty, the devoted search for truth—as especially important clues to the "self-transcending" character of man himself.

Ecstatic humanism seeks, then, to steer a course between explicit religious belief on the one hand and atheistic or reductionistic humanism on the other. It is decidedly a form of humanism in building its outlook upon the best knowledge we have from human reasoning about our experience. But it is a serious and sensitive attention to man in his "self-transcending" characteristics—religion, values, artistic creativity, knowledge and communication, introspection—which opens ecstatic humanism out onto the religious dimension and forbids it from accepting the truncated outlooks of a purely secular humanism. I am arguing, in other words, that an ecstatic or self-transcending humanism is a more fully adequate humanistic position. It is a humanism which recognizes both the limitations of our human situation and knowledge and the mysterious depths and possibilities glimpsed in our human experience.

While the split and vacillation between belief and skepticism have been with me for a number of years, my present "ecstatic humanism" perspective represents a decided shift in my center of gravity. Throughout my undergraduate career and my graduate studies in religion the theist/humanist conflict overwhelmingly resolved itself on the theistic side. Although at one time or another I "tried on" a number of different theological positions, running through them all was a concrete, visible commitment to the Christian faith and the church which expressed itself in ordination to the ministry and a couple of years of part-time parish work. It was researching and writing a doctoral dissertation on the relationship between Dietrich Bonhoeffer's prison writings and his earlier theology[8] which proved to be the turning point for me. With Bonhoeffer I "worked through" my relationship to the Christian tradition and began to turn in broader, more secularized directions. It has been during the years I have spent as a university

25

teacher that I have wrestled with the problems of Christianity from this wider perspective and worked out the open-ended humanistic perspective I now hold.

My relationship to Christianity is now a matter of certain personal hopes arising out of biblical and Christian views of life. Hence I would describe myself as an "ecstatic humanist with Christian hopes." I distinguish sharply here between hope and *faith*, which I take to be a deep-seated *trust* that things are as one believes—for example, that there really is a God who discloses himself to us supremely in Christ. My skepticism prohibits my going that far. I can only speak of certain aspects of the Christian perspective which I very much hope are true. But these hopes, modest as they are, establish my positive and continuing relationship to Christianity and reveal what I consider to be the important contribution of the Hebraic-Christian heritage. As such they are also perhaps informative in disclosing the concerns and problems which underlie the essays in this book.

My "Christian hopes" can be formulated in the following statement: I hope that the transcendent aspect or dimension of reality with which man is in contact in religious experience is characterized by a good purpose which transcends but embraces individual human beings and what they do on this earth. The first half of this statement contains the rational foundation of my hopes. A "transcendent aspect or dimension of reality with which man is in contact in religious experience" I consider to be a not unreasonable possibility in accounting for man's religious experience; that this dimension possesses the characteristics I wish to ascribe to it is a hope based upon the biblical and Christian interpretations of it.

26

I have summarized my specifically Christian-inspired hopes by describing the transcendent dimension of reality as "characterized by a good purpose which transcends but embraces individual human beings and what they do on this earth." I follow the Judaeo-Christian perspective in hoping that the divine is "good" in a sense which is analogous to even as it surpasses what we speak of as "good" in human life: the profound and intimate relationship which can characterize a marriage or a friendship; compassion and self-sacrifice toward persons in need; justice and fair dealing in social relations; the quest for truth; the depths of beauty in both its natural and man-created forms; personal fulfillment; authentic community. Above all, I hope that the transcendent is characterized by that love or *agapē* which Christianity ascribes to it in a singular manner and which seems to me to be the supreme affirmation of the faith founded through Jesus. Again, it must be a love on which we can get a handle through our ordinary experiences of love even though it is far greater, or else talk about the "love of God" becomes nothing but mystery-worship and obfuscation.

Call it egotism, but as long as I am hoping "beyond evidence," I prefer to hope in a God who is genuinely related to, and concerned with, the things human beings care about, a God who makes it worthwhile to seek after the good and redeem the evil as integral elements in a transcendent purpose. Such a God cannot be omnipotent or all-powerful as Christianity traditionally wants him to be; divine omnipotence clashes irreconcilably with that divine love which is the heart and soul of the Christian message. Whether the God in whom I hope is the ultimate reality behind the universe but faced with intractabilities he did not create or perhaps simply one factor out of many in the universe, is a matter for theological speculation. As I see it, all that is necessary is a transcendent aspect or dimension of reality interpreted as caring ultimately for man and unalterably opposed to the evils and sufferings of human life.

In my formulation the adjective "good" modifies the word "purpose." "Purpose" is just such another biblical and Judaeo-Christian notion which is part of my ultimate hopes. My hope is that human life is ultimately purposive in character. By that I mean the hope that individual human lives and human history are going somewhere, that man exists for some end beyond our many proximate ends and other than death and oblivion. The conviction that we are integral episodes in a transcendent drama with its beginning, its middle, and its climax is derived from the faith of Israel, and a breathtaking and affirmative one it is. I find the biblical vision of salvation as the transcendent fulfillment of this world's individual and social human life to be the most religiously adequate view I know, by placing in some meaningful way what means most to human beings within a transcendent purpose. That my concrete struggles, decisions, relationships, achievements, and sufferings and those of other individuals are part and parcel of a higher purpose; that human history is not simply a meaningless rise and fall of nations and empires, wars and pestilences—these hopes seem to me to find their most adequate expression in the biblical faith, for which life is a purposeful pilgrimage to the kingdom of God.

I have already spelled out in large part what I mean by hoping that transcendent reality is characterized by a good purpose "which transcends but embraces individual human beings and what they do on this earth." It is the world-affirmation of biblical and Judaeo-Christian faith (however sorely obscured and frequently compromised by Christianity historically) which is a central element in making its hopes appealing to me.

"Transcends but embraces": This phrase expresses the *dialectical* (yes-and-no) character of the biblical perspective on the world. Life on earth is squarely affirmed because it is seen as integral to God's good purpose; but it is not affirmed, secular-fashion, as an end in itself. This is the dialectical "yes and no" to the world which I have expressed by saying that the divine purpose "transcends but embraces" the world. Such an outlook on the one hand encourages its adherents to take seriously the things we do and care about on earth, because on this view "heaven itself" is made of such things. On the other hand it provides them with (1) a critical principle for man's tendencies to deify himself, his achievements, and his various groups, including his religious institutions; and (2) a fulfillment which rectifies and makes sense of the injustices, sufferings, and aborted goals of this life in a way which straightforward secular humanism cannot do. Point (2) involves the hope of life after death, about which I will have more to say presently.

"Individual human beings and what they do on this earth." This last phrase of my formulation expresses the world affirmation of biblical and Judaeo-Christian faith, which I have already discussed, and also specifies that the good purpose which characterizes transcendent reality has to do with individual persons. The significance of the concrete, personal self as a unique center of meaning and value and a unique object of divine concern came to light historically through the biblical and more particularly the Christian perspective. In the Christian view individual personhood is a unique creation of God, endowed with dignity and offered a destiny all its own. To be sure, in this religious perspective the individual discovers his true individuality, his self, only through community with other persons and ultimately through communion as well with God. That the divine cares about what I am and what every other individual who has ever lived or ever will live is, and has a purpose for each life, is an absolutely mind-stretching notion; but as long as one is hoping, why not?

A divine purpose which "transcends but embraces individual human beings" includes as part of its very logic the hope of life beyond death. To affirm a transcendent good purpose which includes individual persons and their fulfillment and to deny the hope of *post mortem* fulfillment is inconsistent. Just as I consider the hope of life after death to be entailed by the assumptions of Christianity about divine purpose and individual human life, so do I consider the universality of ultimate fulfillment to be entailed by the central Christian affirmation of the divine love. The divine purpose which embraces individual human beings is either all-embracing in bringing all human beings to fulfillment or it is not loving. The whole doctrine of everlasting hell or alienation from God is both inconsistent and offensive in a faith whose burning vision is "grace amazing."

The essays I have collected into this book express some central concerns of mine as one who now views the faith of my upbringing and education from the "borderlands." I have some things of both a critical and a constructive sort also to say on humanism, about which I have already begun to write elsewhere.[9] But in the present essays I address myself to what I believe to be problems contained in some of the chief doctrines of Christian thought: the person and work of Christ; creation "out of nothing," divine omnipotence, and the reality of God; grace and salvation; the resurrection and life after death. At the same time, I explore what I consider to be needed and creative possibilities in Christian thought: a re-examination of the relationship between Jesus and the Christian message; more adequate ways of understanding the relationship between God and the created order; the radical implications of grace; the reaffirmation of Jesus' resurrection and the hope of fulfillment beyond death.

All these issues must sound decidedly "traditional" or "old fashioned" by comparison with many of the timely and "relevant" themes which occupy contemporary theology. But it is precisely my own move from a moderately orthodox position within Christianity to a position on its outskirts which has persuaded me that it is still the "old" problems that bother both the outsider and the perplexed believer. It is precisely certain of the perennially defended and criticized tenets of Christian faith which stubbornly continue to pose to Christianity the most formidable objections to belief. At the same time, it is out of confrontation with some of these venerable and substantial problems that new and creative possibilities of Christian self-understanding and theological development can arise.

I have cut a wide swath in my criticisms, "swinging" at classical and contemporary, conservative and liberal Christian interpretations alike. In the essays on Schweitzer, life beyond death, and the resurrection, I have focused my criticisms especially upon problems of those contemporary approaches to theology which in varying ways and degrees have thought of themselves as "liberal" at least in their positive receptiveness to the impact of modern knowledge upon Christian belief.

While the brunt of my criticisms in the essays on divine omnipotence, the doctrine of creation, and grace is borne by classical or traditional Christian theology, I also show there the remarkable degree to which the ideas I reject as untenable are retained by otherwise "emancipated" twentieth-century theologians.

The opening essay, "Christianity Beyond Christ," broadly (but by no means exhaustively) sets the theme and announces the topics I consider in detail in the rest of the essays. The other essays are arranged in the order in which they are mentioned in the first essay (insofar as they are mentioned there).

Finally, the essays are both independent and interconnected. They were written at various times, most without the others specifically in mind, and each is meant to stand on its own feet. At the same time, they are clearly interwoven both thematically and methodologically. The first two essays belong together; the essays on omnipotence and creation obviously interlock, as do those on eternal life and Jesus' resurrection; the study of grace and salvation links up with several of the other essays. All the essays in various ways hark back to the theme of *agapē* or "amazing grace" as the essence of the Christian proclamation which I enunciate in "Christianity beyond Christ." My method throughout has been twofold: (1) a concern with intellectual coherence and logical implications in Christian thought; and (2) a "radical" or "integral" empiricism which seeks both to be faithful to investigable experience and to resist foreclosing less tractable data such as religious experience and resurrection in a reductionistic manner.

The essays do not necessarily "hang together" as a monolithic outlook. In two essays which touch on the same theme, my emphasis may change from one to the other. Usually this reflects a certain indecision on my part between two or more possibilities which commend themselves. I end up coming down harder now on one alternative and now on the other. At the same time, I have tried to express a unity and consistency of outlook throughout the essays which follow.

I. Christianity Beyond Christ

For some time now I have been intrigued by a passage from William Neil's Preface to the "Knowing Christianity" series:

Organized Christianity is still in its infancy, as is the mind of man as he seeks to grapple with truths that could only come to him by relevation. The half has not yet been told and the full inplications for human thought and action of the coming of God in Christ have as yet been only dimly grasped by most of us.[1]

To this I want to add two statements from Albert Schweitzer's *The Quest of the Historical Jesus* to set the theme of my essay:

It is not Jesus as historically known, but Jesus as spiritually arisen within men, who is significant for our time and can help it. Not the historical Jesus, but the spirit which goes forth from Him and in the spirits of men strives for new influence and rule, is that which overcomes the world.[2]

Jesus means something to our world because a mighty spiritual force streams from Him and flows through our time also. This fact can neither be shaken nor confirmed by any historical discovery. It is the solid foundation of Christianity.[3]

Let me now put together Neil and Schweitzer in the following manner: What is initially disclosed through Jesus is a vision of transcendence which cannot be contained by Jesus, a vision the full implications of which Christians and Christian thinkers are still only beginning dimly to grasp. That vision, held in trust and hope in a frightfully ambiguous world, is best expressed in the simple affirmation of the First Letter of John: "God is love." What decisively comes to light in human experience through the deeds and words of the man Jesus is the stammering but audacious faith that the transcendent mystery with which man has to do is to be characterized as *agapē*—a "will" which universally and unconditionally accepts, heals, purifies, forgives, reconciles, and fulfills.

I want to suggest that this love or (in the words of the familiar hymn) "amazing grace" which is fragmentarily but explosively glimpsed through Jesus is the most adequate criterion of theological thinking. Perhaps such a criterion strikes some readers as self-evident. My point, however, is precisely that it does not seem to have been self-evident throughout the history of Christian thought. It still does not appear to have emerged with full consistency and clarity among theologians, although significant developments have taken place in this direction during the last two centuries.

In one sense, it is true to say that the vision of divine love has always been a central element in Christian life and reflection. All the great theologians, from Paul of Tarsus to Paul Tillich, have been in some way profoundly grasped by *agapē* as the earth-shaking foundation of what is disclosed in Christ. The New Testament, the creeds, the liturgies, the literature of devotion and mysticism—all have been full of proclamation and worship of the God who through Christ is glimpsed as love in his very being. Indeed, the whole power of the Christian message through the centuries has been its "good news" of the drama of salvation: how the Father who throughout eternity loves the Son in the Spirit enables us to share in that love through the incarnation of the Son.

But my whole point is that this vision of the love of God at the center of the gospel has been only partially grasped. One factor has been simply the painfully slow and halting process by which the gospel has leavened human life and history. It is a process, as Professor Neil says, which "is still in its infancy." The other closely related but distinguishable factor has been the obscuring and blurring of the "agapeic vision" by theological considerations themselves. It is to this latter element that I want to devote the remainder of my essay.

What Christian theologians have persistently done, and persist in doing even at the present time, is to allow various other elements in Scripture and theological tradition to compromise Christianity's central vision and its radical implications. Let us look at the foundational case where this has taken place, Christ himself.

It has long been a commonplace of both Roman Catholic and Protestant theology to say that *Christ* is the criterion of biblical interpretation and the norm of theological reflection. In our own day it has been Karl Barth who has proclaimed this with such power and thoroughness. By "Christ" is meant the Figure who confronts us concretely in the New Testament. All extrapolation and speculation about the person and work

36

of Christ, according to most theologians, must be judged in the light of the One whose ministry and meaning are permanently preserved for us in the biblical writings.

Just here is the problem: the problematic character of the biblical Christ himself. I have noticed that most theologians are frankly selective, in considering the biblical Christ, about focusing on those words and deeds of Jesus or interpretations of him which they believe "more truly express who he is." In other words, theologians establish another norm within the great norm of Christ himself. This additional norm, interestingly enough, is almost always (whether implicitly or explicitly) bound up with what I have called the "agapeic vision," although not, it seems to me, in a clear or consistent manner.

Theologians are naturally selective in their use of the biblical figure of Christ because of the formidable difficulties in taking everything he says and does seriously. To put it quite bluntly: What am I to do with a normative Christ whose ministry and self-understanding are so completely bound up with first-century Palestinian Judaism—often in ways we can no longer understand or make use of? who on occasion ties salvation exclusively to his own person? who declares a certain sort of sin "unforgivable"? who at times makes God's forgiveness contingent upon forgiving others? who with grim imagery speaks of the torments of hell? who is flatly mistaken about so crucial an issue as the time of the fulfillment of the kingdom of God? who believes the world is peopled by Satan and his legions of evil spirits? I could go on at considerable length about other similar matters great and small, but these examples will suffice because they and the problem they raise are well known to theologians and to most thoughtful lay people. The problem, of course, is the historical limitations of Jesus.

Ah, I will be told, but this problem is very old hat; nearly all theologians nowadays accept the finite limitations of the man Jesus as a result of historical criticism of the Bible. The trouble, here as elsewhere, is that I find increasingly that it is the "old hat" problems which are the most damaging to the Christian case—*pace* the theologians. The fact is that contemporary theology continues to fail to come to grips with the devastating implications of the limitations and shortcomings of Jesus as historical investigation has been able to disclose them. My point is precisely that it is inconsistent simultaneously to recognize these limitations and shortcomings and to use the biblical Christ as the norm of Christian understanding. What has really happened is that "modern" theologians have seemed reverently to bend the knee before the absoluteness and all-sufficiency of the biblical Christ, while in fact and with varying degrees of awareness they have appealed, rather than to the biblical Christ himself, to a higher norm by which they interpret and evaluate all his uncomfortable and limiting aspects.

To use a celebrated phrase of philosopher Antony Flew from a quite different context which is nevertheless apposite, the "christocentric" norm "dies the death by a thousand qualifications." Theologians begin by taking the biblical Christ as the norm of Christian thinking. Then the objections stemming from his obvious limitations and some of his less-than-agapeic words and actions arise. "Oh yes," they reply, "but we must see that together with this." "But Christ as a full human being shares the limitations of his time and place." "But that passage is not truly expressive of the character of Christ." What began as the supreme criterion finally becomes so hedged about by qualifications which reflect the often surreptitious introduction of another norm that it ceases to be much more than a fine-sounding slogan.

Particularly prominent in contemporary Christian thought is the tendency simply to ignore all the embarrassing passages in the Gospels and Epistles, and in an often breathtaking and breezy fashion to "discover" that the normative Christ is a political revolutionary, a jester, a black, or a therapist. The cultural convenience of all this is obvious; no less so is the careless and highly selective exegesis it involves. Interestingly, it is only the ritual obeisance of theologians to the christocentric norm which makes such interpretations disingenuous and suspect. If theologians would cease being concerned to justify what they consider to be important implications of Christian faith in the twentieth century at the feet of the first-century Christ, they would achieve both consistency and the right to be taken seriously. If agapē and not the biblical Christ were their criterion, the radical implications of Christianity for such matters as social change, race, and psychological conflicts would stand out clearly and cogently.

Conservative Christians have always criticized both liberal and neo-orthodox theologians for saying one thing and doing another when they profess to regard Christ as the criterion of Christian faith and reflection and then use such a free hand with the biblical material. The conservative criticism is entirely justified. It cannot be answered by the kind of maneuvers nonconservative theologians continue to engage in. It could be answered by frankly recognizing that agapē and not the biblical Christ is the proper norm of Christian understanding.

Christian thought is still too tightly grasped and held by theological tradition on this score. The hold needs to be decisively broken by affirming straightforwardly that the gospel is bigger than Christ himself.

A very salutary exercise is to read contemporary theology—indeed, the theology of any period of church history, but markedly and familiarly twentieth-century Christian thought—in the light of the question: Does this make better sense as "obedience to the New Testament Christ" or as "faithfulness to the implications of *agapē* as Christians can perceive it in the present century"? The refreshingly free hand with which the older liberal Protestant thinkers interpreted Christianity, the Niebuhr brothers' stimulating reflections on the relations between Christianity and culture, Bonhoeffer's "nonreligious interpretation," the volumes that continue to pour forth about Christianity and technology, environment, race, sex, politics, revolution—all this reads quite coherently as attempts to apply the logic of the "agapeic vision" to modern life, but rather dubiously and tortuously as christocentric biblical interpretation.

Interestingly enough, it is Albert Schweitzer who among twentieth-century Christian thinkers comes closest to a clear understanding of the issues involved for Christian thinking. The two quotations from *The Quest of the Historical Jesus* at the beginning of this essay are indicative of Schweitzer's approach. He saw, with a candor and courage which have even yet seldom been matched, the degree to which Jesus belongs irrevocably to first-century Palestinian Judaism. It is entirely possible—indeed, necessary—to object to many aspects of Schweitzer's own reconstruction of Jesus, and at the same time to recognize the validity of the questions he still poses to Christian theology.

Schweitzer's enduring insight is his recognition that the spiritual reality and vision unleashed into the world through Jesus of Nazareth break through the bonds of the first century and assume ever-new forms and implications in succeeding generations. Accordingly, Christian reflection is liberated from fixation on the past and free to open itself to the "working of the Spirit" as it unfolds in human life and thought.

It is important to add that for Schweitzer this freedom that belongs to theology does not mean that it loses all connection with the biblical Christ. The job of the theologian in every generation, now greatly aided by knowledge of the historical context of Jesus' mission, is to let himself be confronted by this most spiritually powerful of human figures in all his "pastness," and to glean potentially inexhaustible insights from him in terms of the present age. There is a difference, Schweitzer insisted, between constantly refreshing oneself at the source and wasting one's time being dominated by, or attempting to justify, that source as a final criterion. The latter is the kind of shackling which has characterized not only theology but too much human thought and life: an unnecessary subservience to the past with a consequent reduction of creative possibilities for the present and the future. The creative relationship, according to Schweitzer, lets the past be the past, and precisely by so doing is able again and again to gain the past's wisdom for the present.

Even Schweitzer did not keep his attention riveted steadfastly and consciously on the "agapeic vision" as the norm of Christian thinking with the sense of supreme priority and radical implications which I would wish. But he did see more clearly than most Christian thinkers of our time what it is that comes to light through Jesus, its relationship to Jesus, and its implications for faith and theology.

Like Schweitzer, nothing I have said should be construed as wishing to detract from Jesus himself as the embodiment of the divine *agapē*. Even as a "wondering humanist," and despite the critical difficulties with the New Testament sources, I can only be filled with awe when I ponder the person through whom the incredible vision "God is love" impressed itself with such power upon the minds and hearts of men. Christ is indeed remarkable in his stature as a human being and in his role as the decisive discloser of the "agapeic vision." To say that it is possible and necessary for Christians to see and affirm implications of the vision which Jesus himself did not see and affirm is by no means to rank any later generation with or above him. It is simply to recognize that he embodied the mystery of *agapē* in and through his limitations of time and place and religio-cultural milieu, just as Christians in the latter twentieth century must in trust and hope apprehend the divine love in their partial way and out of their particular experiences and ideas. No amount of development in the unfolding and never-finished grasp of the incredible implications of the "agapeic vision" can take anything away from the towering figure who is the source of it all. One can only return again and again to his words and deeds in the Gospels and to the remarkable interpretations of him in the Epistles with humility and awe as before a presence whose power and mystery defy human categories and turn people's world upside down.

Jesus' words still confront and challenge; they initiate reflection on the "agapeic vision," indict the conscience, and compel to action with dramatic images such as the prodigal son, the lost sheep, the laborers in the vineyard, the command to forgive other persons "not seven times, but seventy times seven." Even more do we see in his deeds the decisive embodiment of *agapē:* his special fellowship with, and compassion for, the poor, the outcast, the neglected; incidents such as the blessing of the children and the forgiving of the woman taken in adultery; his healing of the physically and mentally ill; above all, his sacrificial death, the inexhaustible significance of which the New Testament writings begin profoundly to explore on almost every page. This life and death were in turn surprisingly and shatteringly followed by that mysterious event called the resurrection, the irreducibility of which remains for balanced judgment even after the most critical reading of the texts. The resurrection event itself not only launched the Christian enterprise, but provided Christian reflection with the clue to the meaning of all Christ had been—with a vastly expanded horizon within which to begin to comprehend something of what came to light through this man. If the theology of succeeding centuries must explore ever more widely and deeply the implications of the "agapeic vision," it does so by attending first to, and pondering well, the amazing foundation of it all: this man, this death, this victory.

But press on theologians should if they are to be obedient to the "agapeic vision" which bursts out of the forms in which Christ embodies it. Indeed, we may see his resurrection and the symbol of the pentecostal event—the "coming of the Spirit"—as the basis and justification for Christianity's moving beyond the biblical Christ in its unfolding grasp of the divine love and its implications. The "risen Lord" or "Spirit of Christ" is universalized and free, "calling" every new generation to penetrate ever more deeply into the startling ramifications of this daring faith. Like the impact upon the early followers of Jesus himself, openness to new and unexpected possibilities is of the very essence of that Hebraic heritage for which God is always "doing a new thing."

With its in principle excellent central notion that Christian doctrine is a living, "organic" development intimately bound up with the ongoing, changing life of the Christian community, the Roman Catholic tradition might be expected to be able best to understand and appreciate the viewpoint I am commending. We find among some of its most liberal spokesmen at the present time some of the most exciting explorations in this general direction to be found anywhere, although they continue to understand their reflections in christocentric terms. I am thinking chiefly of theologians such as Father Gregory Baum in his remarkable book *Man Becoming*.[4]

However, the idea of doctrinal development in Roman Catholicism is still officially—and to a very large degree unofficially—tied to a deeply conservative understanding of the normativity of Christ and of the biblical documents. It is at this point that Protestant thought, with its now long-standing tradition in many quarters of creative openness to criticism and revision in the light of the modern advance of knowledge, might be expected to be more receptive to the picture of the "essence of Christianity" which I am commending. Indeed, insofar as I relate myself to Christianity and Christian theology, I tend to find my own deepest kinship with the liberal Protestant tradition. Albeit with varying degrees of awareness and consistency, the great liberal thinkers seem to have had the firmest grasp on what is

44

at stake for Christian self-understanding as a result of our knowledge of Christian origins.

I want now to mention briefly what I believe to be a few of the important doctrinal implications of the "agapeic vision" which Christian theology can and ought to affirm with the light available to it at this point in the slow and fitful "coming of age" of Christianity throughout that history designated "A.D." I feel more confident about some of the directions the trusting hope that "God is love" should lead Christian thought than I do about others. Sometimes I can see possibilities in working out the entailments of *agapē* with the always partial and fragmentary knowledge which is man's situation vis-à-vis the transcendent. Some readers will quarrel with some of my "deductions" and offer their own. All this is as it should be. Theology, like faith itself, is always risk, venture into the darkness with a few flickering candles. Theology, like faith itself, is always a shared enterprise in which persons enrich and correct one another out of the rich diversity of individual perceptions. Furthermore, each of my points demands considerable elaboration and discussion which I cannot introduce here.

The problem of evil. Most theologians still insist upon the omnipotence and omniscience of God, together with their corollary, *creatio ex nihilo* or the total dependence of everything created upon the Creator. Since on this view the only limitations on God are self-imposed, I have concluded after considerable wrestling with the standard doctrine that this view cannot escape the conclusion that God is ultimately responsible for moral and physical evil. Such a conclusion appears to me to be simply unacceptable in the light of the "agapeic vision," which demands that the divine love be the unequivocal foe and not the source or condition of evil.

It seems to me that Christian faith and theology must choose either to be faithful to the logic of *agapē* and deny the divine omnipotence and creation "out of nothing"; or to continue to compromise the "agapeic vision" rather seriously by making God finally responsible for evil. To choose the former has decided consequences for the Christian understanding of God, and to this I want now to turn.

The reality of God. The problem of evil forces Christianity, I believe, radically to rethink its traditional ways of thinking about the God of love. A God who is sharply set over against evil as its antithesis and overcomer may simply stand in intolerable tension with the omnipotent, omniscient "ground of being." Biblical faith (and practical Christianity, for that matter) begins and finds its living sustenance in the experience of a Reality transcending man and his environment, which purges, heals, and liberates. Why must Christian theology persist in asking for more? Here Bultmann's rigorously existential and "anthropological" approach to faith hits the mark squarely: God known is "God-for-us"; anything more is speculation. Happily, one recent theological trend, represented by thinkers such as Gregory Baum in *Man Becoming,* has in other ways been calling faith and theology resolutely back from the cosmic to the earthly, from the Supreme Being to the liberating presence in human life.

Faithfulness to the implications of *agapē* may demand an agnostic silence about the relationship of the divine reality to the cosmos as a whole. Any speculation beyond this must, it seems to me, be frankly open to dualism or pluralism in interpreting God relative to

46

the universe. The transcendent love which Christians believe is experienced by man is at least a "depth-dimension," a real force or "will" within reality which is experienced as enduring and triumphant. Is it really a disaster if in affirming the "living God," the creative transcendent within human life and history, Christians are driven to reject the omnipotent Creator? Contrary to some recent theological pleas (inspired, for example, by the work of Pierre Teilhard de Chardin) for renewed affirmation of the cosmic Creator, I would argue that in the light of *agapē* it may be that "your God is too big."

Salvation. This doctrine is a chief sore point in Christianity which should instead be one of its most powerful affirmations. Much freeing up has taken place in this area for recent Christian thought, but it is time for nonconservative theologians to stop all hedging and qualifying and unequivocally affirm the universal salvation of all human beings. There can be no other conclusion, as I see it, when the vision of God as love is pondered in the light of the implications which Christian believers in the twentieth century are able to grasp. If the transcendent aspect of reality with which Christianity believes man is in touch is truly a "will" whose ceaseless purpose is to reconcile and reunite, then everlasting hell is both insufferable and illogical. All the nice, ostensibly reasonable defenses of everlasting alienation, from Augustine to C. S. Lewis, in the final analysis create irreconcilable anomalies within the "agapeic vision."

Christians have far too many inherited hang-ups in this area which prevent them from joyously proclaiming the incredible message that makes Christianity Good News, that expresses purely and simply the vision of love abounding underneath the often dark and ugly rid-

47

dles of existence: None is ultimately lost; all are finally healed, forgiven, reconciled, reunited, fulfilled. The transcendent "will" which manifests itself in human life binds up and gathers to itself all human beings in a destiny far beyond our comprehension but foreshadowed or "parabolized" in our fragmentary experiences of compassion, succor, interpersonal union, beauty, and truth. This is Good News; this is hope in an often strange and confusing world; this is a grand vision worthy of the faith which asserts that "God is love."

These represent some of the crucial theological areas which seem to me to require further revising and "liberating" in the light of the vision of *agapē* which I would maintain is the distinctive essence of Christianity. The kind of alteration and freeing up which is needed will in turn require *metanoia* (repentance) with respect to some hard-dying traditions of theological compromise, above all the normativity of the biblical Christ. It will require a constant purification of Christian thinking by steadfast attention to the "agapeic vision" itself and refusal to absolutize any of its particular historical expressions. In their recalling of the church to essentials, the Protestant Reformers and their theological descendants have not gone far enough. Not "Scripture alone," not "faith alone," not even "Christ alone"—but "love alone" is the proper norm of Christian understanding.

II. Albert Schweitzer on Theological Uses and Abuses of the Historical Jesus

Albert Schweitzer's thought moved back and forth between the two poles of historical investigation and theological reflection. His characteristic method, whether he was studying primitive Christianity or philosophical ethics, was (1) to do a historical survey of the work done on the same subject up to his time; [1] (2) to undertake his own historical investigation; and (3) to put forward, on the basis of his own and his predecessors' historical study, theological suggestions of a creative but often unclearly defined sort.[2]

Analysis of Schweitzer's historical understanding and theological reflections, with chief attention to the relation between the two, seems to me to be one of the most illuminating approaches to his thought. Examination of these two foci reveals that the Schweitzer corpus is not so theologically amorphous as it appears on the surface, but rather possesses a fundamental unity of purpose. At the same time, however, it shows that he failed to think through his position with sufficient clarity or thoroughness, which resulted in a certain incoherence and vagueness of expression. Finally, a study of the relation between historical study and theological reflection in Schweitzer's thought discloses him to be a religious thinker who trod his own singular and arresting way to the end of his active career, standing aside from, and in criticism of, those trends which have dominated twentieth-century theology.

1. Historical Understanding

It is clear from Schweitzer's writings that the possibility of a critically objective, relatively presuppositionless historical science is a foundation stone of his intellectual outlook. He discusses his concept of historical investigation most fully in a section of Part I of *The Philosophy of Civilization*.[3] Here he introduces the subject as part of a scathing criticism of the "irrationality" of the thought of his time. The thrust of his argument is that history-writing in the early twentieth century, for all its scholarly advantages, has too often become subservient to present needs such as propaganda. History, Schweitzer objects, is studied by his generation not to understand the past but to justify the present. As a result, not only is history distorted, but the present remains irrationally dominated by the past rather than by reason. Schweitzer places this "artificial" relationship to the past over against a "normal" one, in which the past is allowed to be the past.[4]

"Historical sense, in the full meaning of the term," Schweitzer writes, "implies a critical objectivity in the face of far-off and recent events alike."[5] His criticism of contemporary historians further indicates his adherence to this view of historical investigation:

> It is significant that while during the last few decades [1890-1920] the learning of our historians has, no doubt, increased, their critical objectivity has not. Previous investigators kept this ideal before their eyes in much greater purity than have those of to-day; we have gone so far that we no longer seriously make the demand that in scientific dealings with the past there shall be a suppression of all prejudices which spring from nationality or creed. It is quite common nowadays to see the greatest learning bound up with the strongest bias. In our historical literature the highest positions are occupied by works written with propagandist aims.[6]

When we recall that *The Philosophy of Civilization* was written during and immediately following World War I, a period when religion, scholarship, and everything else climbed aboard the bandwagons of nationalist propaganda, Schweitzer's words here must be seen not only as his warning to every generation of historians, but also as a highly critical "tract for the times."

At one point in *The Quest of the Historical Jesus,* Schweitzer criticizes a certain method of reconstructing the life of Jesus as inconsistent with "pure objective history." [7] The historian, by virtue of his rationality, is capable of detaching himself sufficiently from the limitations of time, place, and ideological and personal prejudice, to examine historical evidence impartially and to reconstruct the past faithfully. Data about the past are a "given," somewhat like the data of the natural sciences, and can be examined by what are fundamentally scientific and rational methods. Schweitzer recognized that historical science entails a larger degree of subjective factors than the natural sciences, and that

51

the "givenness" of its data differs from the "givenness" of the data of the natural sciences in being "once-for-all" rather than repeatable. He nevertheless believed it possible, given the nature of its data, for historical investigation to attain a high degree of objectivity appropriate to its sphere of inquiry.

Schweitzer intended that history-writing be as single-minded as possible. Nowhere is he more insistent about this than in the case of religious historians or theologians who turn to history. *The Quest of the Historical Jesus* is full of sharp criticisms of the demonstrable distortions of the history behind the four Gospels by "dogmatic historians" who insist upon regarding New Testament study as an exercise in theological apologetic rather than as objective historical inquiry. The Christian historian, involved in a theological tradition, is nevertheless called upon as a historian to set his dogmatic framework and apologetic interest entirely aside.

Schweitzer meant to be a rationalist somewhat in the manner of eighteenth-century Enlightenment thought, for which he had high admiration. The ability to investigate the past with critical objectivity was for Schweitzer a clear example of the supra-historical character of reason. Although the mind is limited by historical factors, there is an essence of rationality which transcends historical factors; it is this supra-historical capacity of thinking which enables a Schweitzer, for example, to read and understand a Plato. Reason expresses supra-historical truth in historical forms, such as the late-Jewish eschatology in which Jesus embodied what Schweitzer considered to be certain timeless truths of reason; but it is also capable of abstraction, of getting behind the historical forms to the universal truth of the matter.

In his view of the supra-historical character of reason and the corollary possibility of objective historical study, Schweitzer represented the viewpoint of many liberal Protestant religious thinkers of the nineteenth and early twentieth centuries. What is not usually noticed, when Schweitzer's outlook is classed as a variety of the ascendant liberalism, is the way in which he radically criticized and moved beyond his generation of liberals on the basis of the very premises which they all shared concerning reason and history. In a manner less systematic and more isolated, Schweitzer's critique of liberalism from within must stand alongside the more impressive efforts of Ernest Troeltsch.

The rise of modern critical historical investigation of the Bible in the nineteenth century was bravely seized upon by those Protestant scholars whom we call "liberal" because of their attempts, in varying degrees, to bring Christian belief into conformity with the new scientific and historical knowledge. A chief interest among these scholars was what is usually called "life-of-Jesus research." They reasoned that the new critical-historical methods enabled us for the first time to reconstruct Jesus as he really was, to peel away the layers of mythology and doctrine in which the New Testament writings veil him and get at the flesh-and-blood human being. The liberals believed that this was an inestimable gain for Christianity. Christian faith and theology could now be solidly grounded in historical data —in facts available to open historical investigation— rather than in obscure dogmas and incredible myths which the modern mind rightly considered dubious in the light of nineteenth-century knowledge. The Christian could make his appeal to public historical knowledge of the man Jesus. He differed from the nonbeliever only in his "value judgment," as the influential theologian Albrecht Ritschl called it, that what was disclosed through this historical figure was the clue to the meaning of human life and the cosmos.

What Schweitzer graphically exposed in *The Quest of the Historical Jesus* was the degree to which the results of nineteenth-century life-of-Jesus research reflected the intrusion of the researchers' modern religious and cultural presuppositions into the historical data. The historical Jesus turned out conveniently in case after case to be a man with whom any nineteenth-century European moralist would have felt comfortable. He was seen as having used the prevailing first-century religious beliefs of his fellow Jews simply as the natural medium through which to communicate a message which he knew they could not adequately contain. Many of Jesus' strange sayings and doings were explained away as inventions of the early Christian community, which was believed to be still dominated by the prevailing milieu of Jewish beliefs and expectations.

The eminent church historian Adolf Harnack's immensely popular book *What Is Christianity?* was perhaps the most influential and responsible of these liberal life-of-Jesus efforts. Yet Schweitzer could write in *The Quest of the Historical Jesus:* "Harnack, in his 'What is Christianity?' almost entirely ignores the contemporary limitations of Jesus' teaching, and starts out with a Gospel which carries him down without difficulty to the year 1899." Schweitzer goes on to call this procedure "anti-historical violence." [8] Harnack was trying to do both historical investigation and theological reconstruction in *What Is Christianity?* On the basis of his historical researches into Jesus and the origins of Christianity, he sought to uncover the timeless, permanent "essence of Christianity" (the original German title of the book is *Das Wesen des Christentums*) within its historical forms—the enduring kernel within the temporary husk.

It was not Harnack's understanding of the task of theology to which Schweitzer objected. As we shall see in Section 2, Schweitzer himself saw the task of theology as creative reflection on the supra-historical or "rational" essence of Christianity which first came to expression in the words and deeds of Jesus. Harnack's error, which was representative of the liberal life-of-Jesus approach, lay in *ascribing to Jesus himself this distinction between the enduring substance and its historical accidents.* This was the chief point of disagreement between Schweitzer and other Protestant liberals. Their differences lay not so much in their theological conclusions as in the way they related their conclusions to the historical knowledge of Christian origins. For Harnack and the other influential Jesus-researchers of the latter nineteenth century, their distillation of what they considered to be the "eternal message" of Christianity out of its first-century Jewish forms was grounded in the attitude of Jesus himself. Jesus, they maintained, saw through the religious beliefs and mythological perspectives which formed the very air he breathed as a Palestinian Jew. Jesus himself sat lightly to all the prevailing talk about eschatology, apocalypse, demon possession, and the like, and sovereignly bent them to his own timeless uses. Harnack went so far as to say that "Jesus Christ's teaching will at once bring us by steps which, if few, will be great, to a height where its connexion with Judaism is seen to be only a loose one, and most of the threads leading from it into 'contemporary history' become of no importance at all." [9]

It was precisely this assumption that Schweitzer exposed and attacked in *The Quest of the Historical Jesus.* It was a clear case, he believed, of importing modern presuppositions into historical investigation of Jesus and thereby distorting the facts. Schweitzer tried to show, by contrast, what a thoroughly first-century Jew the New Testament revealed Jesus to be, how deeply he shared the beliefs and expectations of his people, and accordingly how strange he is to us in many respects if we look at him honestly as a historical figure. For Schweitzer, then, the door was closed by historical investigation just as firmly to liberal religious ideas as it was to traditional orthodox doctrines, insofar as they sought to base themselves upon the Jesus of history.

Schweitzer's exposure of the liberal "lives of Jesus" for importing theological assumptions into historical investigation is a manifestation of what we have seen to be his general insistence that the study of history is capable of greater scientific detachment and objectivity than his fellow liberals, who paid lip service to the idea, were willing to practice. When the chips were down, Schweitzer believed, historical honesty gave way to theological demands for the liberal no less than for the orthodox; uncomfortable or theologically irreconcilable aspects of the historical Jesus were suppressed or explained away.

Even more important in terms of understanding his own theology is Schweitzer's corollary belief that the attempt of liberal Protestant scholars such as Ritschl and Harnack to reconstruct theology on the basis of what they considered to be objective historical investigation of the New Testament reflected an incorrect understanding of the relation between historical science and theological reflection—an error which inevitably expressed itself in their conscious or unconscious subordination of historical fact to modern theological motives and interpretations. It is precisely a proper understanding of the past, and of the relation between the past and the essential capacity of reason to transcend its historical forms, Schweitzer argued, which the attempt at a truly objective study of history brings to light. It is furthermore this clear-sighted apprehension of the past and its relation to the supra-historical essence of reason which suggests the appropriate path for theological reflection. In the next section we shall consider how Schweitzer developed this notion of theology.

2. Theological Reflection

"In genuine historical knowledge there is liberating and helping power." This statement from Schweitzer's early book *The Mystery of the Kingdom of God* provides our discussion with a succinct transition from history to theology.[10] It will be recalled that Schweitzer criticized his generation of historians and theologians for using historical knowledge to justify themselves rather than to understand the past. The result of this misuse of the past is an "artificial" relationship to history which is characterized by the subservience of the present to the past. It is an axiom with Schweitzer that the tyranny of the past is directly proportional to the attempt to use it primarily to justify the present. Conversely, genuine historical knowledge, which allows the past simply to be the past, liberates the present from the past and allows the present to create its own destiny. Only a rigorously objective and critical approach to the past, freed as far as humanly possible from contemporary presuppositions, can insure this freedom for the present.

Schweitzer's theology can be understood only if this rationalist approach to history is given full recognition. Here also his corollary concept of reason as essentially supra-historical must be integrally included. Human reason transcends history in its essential nature. Hence it must never let itself be tyrannized by the past. Every generation must find the truth for itself in its own historical forms; every age must discover its motivating ideas and teleological ideals afresh. Schweitzer's view of the intrinsic independence of reason from history appeals frankly to the "unhistorical" rationalism of the eighteenth century.[11]

In *The Philosophy of Civilization* Schweitzer deplores the subservience of the present to the past in the sphere of religion:

> It is because Oriental and Greek conceptions which have had their day are still current among us that we bleed to death over problems which otherwise would have no existence for us. How much we suffer from the one fact that to-day and for several centuries past our thoughts about religion have been under the hereditary foreign domination of Jewish transcendentalism and Greek metaphysics, and, instead of being able to express themselves naturally, have suffered continual distortion![12]

The present must instead study the past faithfully and learn from it on its own terms; it must let it be what it is in truth and not force it into the mold of authority over, or justification of, the present. Only in this way is the present free from the past and productive of new ideas. "It is from new ideas that we must build history anew." [13]

Schweitzer carries over this attitude into theology; indeed, it is his theological reflections which spell it out most fully. "Religion," he says, "has . . . no reason for trying to avoid coming to terms with historical truth." [14] Here we have Schweitzer's basic platform for both his historical and his theological work.

Remarking on the liberative power of historical study for theology, Schweitzer states: "Genuine historical knowledge . . . restores to theology full freedom of movement." [15] A fuller statement follows which may be taken as Schweitzer's delineation of the theological task:

Therefore may modern theology, just by reason of a genuine historical knowledge, claim freedom of movement, without being hampered continually by petty historical expedients which nowadays are often resorted to at the expense of historical veracity. Theology . . . is free, for its task is to found our Christian view of the world solely upon the personality of Jesus Christ, *irrespective of the form in which it expressed itself in his time.* He himself has destroyed this form with his death. *History prompts theology to this unhistorical step.*[16]

Three things should be observed in this crucial statement:

(1) Theology is properly a "free" mode of inquiry, by which Schweitzer means that it is "unhistorical." The work of the theologian is not bound to certain problematic historical events for its content and justification.

(2) It is historical investigation itself which enables theology to be free—i.e., to be "unhistorical." In fact, Schweitzer is saying, it is the historical investigation of the origins of Christianity which *demands* that theology

be freed from the past. Schweitzer's own rigorous and thoroughgoing eschatological interpretation of Jesus revealed (as far as he was concerned) that the life and teaching of Christianity's founder were expressed in a historically conditioned form which we can never appropriate as our own. Honest historical inquiry thus releases Christian theology from the obligation to try to fit Jesus' world view into ours, or vice versa.

(3) Jesus' "personality" may be equated with his "spirit" or even with his "reason"—which in his theological reflections Schweitzer uses in a broad, extremely vague sense. This "spirit" of Jesus is separable from the historical forms in which it was expressed. A favorite theme of Schweitzer's is the idea that Jesus' death, destroying as it did his eschatological belief that the Messiah's death would force the coming of the kingdom of God, released his spirit (i.e., his personality) from historical limitation into supra-historical universality:

> With his death he destroyed the form of his *Weltanschauung*, rendering his own eschatology impossible. *Thereby he gives to all peoples and to all times the right to apprehend him in terms of their thoughts and conceptions*, in order that his spirit may pervade their "Weltanschauung" as it quickened and transfigured the Jewish eschatology.[17]

The task of theology is to get behind the historical forms in which the ethical personality or spirit of Jesus expressed itself to the timeless, supra-historical essence of the Christ.

The theological distillation of the eternal personality or spirit of Jesus out of its historical container is the dominant and consistent theme of Schweitzer's theological work. In *The Quest of the Historical Jesus* he writes:

It is not given to history to disengage that which is abiding and eternal in the being of Jesus from the historical forms in which it worked itself out, and to introduce it into our world as a living influence. . . . *The abiding and eternal in Jesus is absolutely independent of historical knowledge and can only be understood by contact with His spirit which is still at work in the world.*[18]

The above passage also expresses Schweitzer's fundamental criticism of the dominant liberal Protestant theology of his day: its erroneous assumption "that we could build up by the increase of historical knowledge a new and vigorous Christianity." [19] That, says Schweitzer, is not the task of historical investigation; such an approach in fact distorts historical investigation. It is the theological version of the more general attitude toward the past which Schweitzer so deplores, in which the past is not allowed to be itself but is subtly, often half-consciously, interpreted in such a way as to make it agree with a particular contemporary outlook. Ritschl and Harnack tried to make historical science do what it was not intended to do. A truly free theology, Schweitzer insisted, is alive to the independence of "spirit" or "reason" from its historical expressions.

Schweitzer's separation of the supra-historical from the historical appears also in his interpretation of the apostle Paul's Christ-mysticism:

This Christ-Mysticism Paul thought out within the framework of the eschatological world-view, with such depth and living power that, so far as its spiritual content is concerned, it remains valid for all aftertimes. As a fugue of Bach's belongs in form to the eighteenth century, but in its essence is pure musical truth, so does the Christ-mysticism of all times find itself again in the Pauline as its primal form.[20]

For Schweitzer, Christianity *is* Christ-mysticism; and Christ-mysticism is participation in the eternal spirit of Jesus. This is the abiding content behind all the outward historical forms of Christianity. The illustration from Bach is significant—if typically obscure—because it shows that Schweitzer extends this historical/suprahistorical distinction into other areas of thought.

Again, Schweitzer employs the theological method of "supra-historical distillation" in a very important chapter of *Out of My Life and Thought*, entitled "The Historical Jesus and the Christianity of Today":

> So far as its essential spiritual and ethical nature is concerned, Christianity's religious truth remains the same throughout the centuries. The variations belong only to the outward form which it assumes in the ideas belonging to different world-views.[21]

The first of these "variations" belonging only to "the outward form" was, of course, Jesus' own consciousness as a first-century Jewish eschatological figure. Schweitzer reveals the full extent of his supra-historical conception of Christianity when he says: "The ideal would be that Jesus should have preached religious truth in a form independent of any connection with any particular period and such that it could be taken over simply and easily by each succeeding generation of men."[22] There is another side to Schweitzer's theological reflections which appears to be inconsistent with the above. In reality, however, it further expresses his understanding of history and its relation to theology. We have seen that for Schweitzer the past has a creative and helpful effect on the present only when it is allowed to be what it really was. Only when the present can view the past critically and objectively, at a distance, is the present free to use the past creatively and not servilely. Applied to theology this produces the following proposition: *It is precisely by letting the life and the words of Jesus be what they really were that they are freed to speak to every generation with power.* When we no longer attempt to read into Jesus' words the meanings encrusted upon them by tradition and dogma or even by the "modern" presuppositions of liberal scholars in their "quest of the historical Jesus," they become ever new vehicles of his spirit—i.e., of the timeless essence of Christianity. Historical investigation has enabled us to clear away the debris and to confront the historical Jesus and his teaching in all their starkness and strangeness. Although we can never appropriate the historical forms which make Jesus so foreign to us, those very forms—especially his words— convey by their very strangeness and radicalness the eternal truth of Christianity. The supra-historical essence is discovered in its primordial power by each generation simply by confronting the demands of Jesus' teaching and life as recorded in the Gospels. It is by remaining historically "irrelevant" that the historical Jesus becomes theologically "relevant."

This approach to the historical as the vehicle of the supra-historical appears in *The Quest of the Historical Jesus:*

Jesus as a concrete historical personality remains a stranger to our time, but His spirit, which lies hidden in His words, is known in simplicity, and its influence is direct. Every saying contains in its own way the whole Jesus. *The very strangeness and unconditionedness in which He stands before us makes it easier for individuals to find their own personal standpoint in regard to Him.*[23]

Schweitzer believes that the key to this phenomenon lies in the very eschatology which totally removes Jesus from the modern view of Jesus:

That which is eternal in the words of Jesus is due to the very fact that they are based on an eschatological world-view, and contain the expression of a mind for which the contemporary world with its historical and social circumstances no longer had any existence. They are appropriate, therefore, to any world, for in every world they raise the man who dares to meet their challenge, and does not turn and twist them into meaninglessness, above his world and his time, making him inwardly free, so that he is fitted to be, in his own world and in his own time, a simple channel of the power of Jesus.[24]

The encounter with the supra-historical directly through the historical is made even more explicit in *Out of My Life and Thought:* "whoever preaches . . . the Gospel of Jesus must settle for himself what the original meaning of His sayings was, and work his way up through the historical truth to the eternal." [25] Speaking directly to the central theological reality, the "personality" or "spirit" of Jesus, Schweitzer says:

Even if the historical Jesus has something strange about Him, yet His personality, as it really is, influences us much more strongly and immediately than when He approached us in dogma and in the results attained up to the present by research. . . .

Anyone who ventures to look the historical Jesus straight in the face and to listen for what He may have to teach Him in his powerful sayings, soon ceases to ask what this strange-seeming Jesus can still be to him.[26]

Schweitzer's position on the spiritual significance of the past can be summed up in a statement from *The*

Mysticism of Paul the Apostle: "The permanent spiritual importance that the religious thought of the past has for ours makes itself most strongly felt when we come into touch with that form of piety as it really existed, not as we make the best of it for ourselves." [27] In all areas of life, it is precisely the free and critical confrontation with the past on its own terms which alone gives the past enduring relevance.

3. Some Observations

What can be said by way of evaluation of Schweitzer's understanding of historical investigation and theology and their relationship? I want to suggest a few criticisms, both negative and positive. First on the minus side:

While I have sought to illuminate the basic unity and consistency of Schweitzer's overall historical and theological outlook, it is clear that when we get down to specifics of conceptuality and terminology, of argument and exposition, he is frustratingly vague and sometimes even incoherent. We have a right, I think, to expect a certain rigor and precision from a man who thought of himself as a rationalist, but we do not find it in Schweitzer. When he moves, for example, from historical investigation to theological reflection his concept of "reason" becomes amorphously broad and elusive. Within his theological thinking, we are never quite sure we have a handle on Schweitzer's quasimystical, cryptic references to "spirit" and "the eternal." Schweitzer was in many ways an intuitive person in his apprehension of life; furthermore, he was strongly influenced by music and by mysticism. Because of these things, there is a certain deliberateness about his terminological vagueness and lack of carefulness, a conviction (which he shares with some other distinguished thinkers) that such basic concepts as "reason," "spirit," and "the eternal" are words pointing open-endedly to a never fully determinate reality rather than denotations of definite content. Yet he never really comes out and states this basically unobjectionable premise; nor does he recognize that even within such an open-ended use of key concepts there are specific things which can be said and limits which can be defined; and finally, he makes not even a minimal effort in his usage to avoid inconsistency and sheer obscurity. In short, Schweitzer as a constructive religious thinker lacked the discipline which adds useful clarity and communicability to creative insight.

On the matter of historical objectivity the advantage of hindsight enables us to see the overconfidence of Schweitzer's generation of historians. The research done on the historical Jesus since *The Quest of the Historical Jesus*, with its revolutionary methods, its improved data, and its nevertheless bewildering variety of equally tenable conclusions, is a very apt illustration. Almost no one today accepts Schweitzer's reconstruction of the historical Jesus or the methodology by which he approached the data—although we are all in his lasting debt for the dramatic and rigorous way in which he forced upon us the fact that Jesus was indeed a thoroughly first-century Jew and an eschatological figure. But neither is anyone today confidently prepared to set a clear alternative in its place as "the" historical Jesus. The further development of life-of-Jesus research, like further developments in historical investigation generally, has made us considerably more modest and tentative. We recognize more clearly now not only the selectiveness and arbitrariness of what is preserved to us from the past, but also—and very importantly relative to Schweitzer—the selective and interpretative involvement of the historian in his research and data. Schweitzer and his contemporaries were certainly aware of the subjective factors in historical investigation, but they tended to be dominated by the positivistic model taken from the reigning natural sciences, and therefore assumed a higher degree of detachment and objectivity than we can today. Significantly, of course, it is precisely our more chastened and self-conscious recognition of the limitations of historical science which makes for a higher degree of genuine "objectivity" in reconstructing the past than was possible for an age which was less keenly aware of these limitations.

But on this very matter of historical objectivity we must turn to the positive side of our appraisal of Schweitzer. If it is necessary to point out against Schweitzer the limitations of historical objectivity, it is at the same time necessary to insist along with him that historical investigation must constantly strive for as high a degree of objectivity as is possibile within these limitations. Whatever criticisms we may have today of Schweitzer's specific methods and conclusions in studying the historical Jesus, he stands out from among even the liberal religious historians of his time in his rigorous and single-minded concern to be historically honest come what may. Schweitzer rightly insisted that the historian must discipline himself stringently to set aside, so far as humanly possible, his own religious, political, and personal views in order to let the evidence we have from the past speak for itself. For the Christian historian of the New Testament, this means clearly recognizing and detaching himself as much as he can from his own most cherished beliefs as well as those of church tradition, and facing unflinchingly what he as a historian finds out about Jesus. It was Schweitzer's own intellectual honesty as a historian which made *The Quest of the Historical Jesus* a watershed in modern historical study of Jesus. Although others preceded him in pointing both to the apologetic and "modernizing" tendencies of life-of-Jesus researchers and to the dominance of eschatology in Jesus' ministry and message, it was Schweitzer who meticulously documented the former and unforgettably dramatized the latter in such a way that all future historians of Christian origins have had to face these issues squarely.

Schweitzer's high standards of historical objectivity represent a permanent challenge to the Christian historian of the New Testament. Equally important, however, is the challenge for the Christian theologian. Schweitzer saw much more clearly than most of his fellow liberals the disturbing implications for Christian faith and theology of modern historical investigation of Christian origins. Furthermore, as we have seen, he articulated the problem (if not a solution) in such a stark and vigorous manner as still to command our attention and disturb us. Among later theologians the name of Rudolf Bultmann comes prominently to mind as another who has also raised unrelentingly the historical problem which the theologian must face; significantly, he is a New Testament historian. If Bultmann has explored the dilemma with better methodological tools, greater thoroughness, and more nearly acceptable conclusions, Schweitzer must nevertheless stand alongside him as a vigorous critic of the theological uses of history.[28]

There is something of crucial and lasting importance to be gained from Schweitzer's understanding of the relationship between historical investigation and theology. His insistence upon their independence from each other, whatever quarrels we may have with the details of his argument, contains devastating insights which some of the most influential forms of Protestant theology have by and large not yet confronted. Historical criticism of the New Testament has done a reasonably conscientious job of putting theological presuppositions to one side or at least of recognizing their involvement in the investigation, although constant vigilance is still needed in this area. But many theologians who have accepted with Schweitzer the problematic character of the historical Jesus still tend to be unable to look squarely at the issue which Schweitzer saw and articulated so clearly and which further developments in New Testament criticism have only intensified—the problem of the relationship between the historical Jesus and Christian faith.

Schweitzer's *The Quest of the Historical Jesus* and its related works stand before us still asking the same telling questions about the relation of the historical Jesus to Christian theology: Is it not in the last analysis impossible to build Christian theology upon the "real" Jesus, this first-century Palestinian Jew who moved entirely within the current Jewish mythology and believed the world would soon end (two central aspects of Schweitzer's analysis which have not been seriously questioned)? Furthermore: Is it even desirable, even if we fool ourselves into thinking it is possible, to try to base Christian theology upon Jesus? However much we may quarrel with Schweitzer's methodology or with details of his historical reconstruction, he confronted us dramatically with the extent to which Jesus himself and some of what he said are simply strange and foreign to us. It seems to me that twentieth-century Jesus-research has tended only to reinforce Jesus' distance from us, to which it has added through form criticism his perplexing historical inaccessibility to us, available as he is only through the faith documents of a religious community. Mention of the work of Bultmann suffices as a central and influential example.

Since the rise of the historical study of the Bible, as Schweitzer rightly pointed out, theologians have resorted to all sorts of expedients in an effort to mitigate, ignore, leap over, or "fudge" this fundamental fact of the historical limitations and relative inaccessibility of Jesus. Given the situation of modern historical consciousness and the tools of critical historical investigation, many liberal as well as neo-orthodox theologians have nevertheless by and large continued to assume without much thorough analysis or consistency that Christian theology must justify Jesus as the norm of Christian thinking, no matter how enigmatic or irrelevant some aspects of the man are; and conversely, that theological ideas in the twentieth or any other century must be made to look as if they express what Jesus or the "biblical faith" "really" say or mean. It is no small portion of Schweitzer's permanent legacy that he had the intellectual honesty and the spiritual independence to question this whole understanding of the theological task as either unconsidered or dishonest.

The "death of God" theologians point to the "loss of transcendence" in the modern world and find in the New Testament the picture of the man who in his life and death is the self-emptying of the transcendent into the world; the analysts of secularity find in the

biblical outlook an ancient healthy-minded affirmative-
ness about life and a view of God which potentially
"de-divinizes" the world and lets it be autonomous; the
"theologians of hope" find in the eschatological dynamic
of Jesus and early Christianity permanent implications
for an attitude of active openness to the future characterized by an active concern for social justice and
compassion. Each of these recent theological movements
has uncovered highly fruitful insights at the Christian
source into decisive phenomena of our time. But is it
necessary to insist, with one-sided exegesis and other
contortions, that this is what the Bible and Jesus
"really" mean? They mean a lot of other things, too,
some of which are totally irrelevant to our time. If
there are, in the remembered and interpreted Jesus of
the New Testament, creative implications for modern
thought and perspectival criteria which aid in illuminating and assessing our age, that represents an important theological contribution to our knowledge and our
attitudes. The theologian is the person to bring them
to our attention and to turn the Christian community
in these needed directions. But the attempt to "justify
Jesus to the world and the world to Jesus" has become
in modern theology, with its full knowledge of the
historical problems surrounding the sources of Christianity, an artificial and tendentious exercise. If insights are believed to be consistent with the Christian
vision of divine love as it has unfolded down to this
point in history, they can stand on that basis; they
do not need the additional sanction and authority of
"what Jesus really meant to say or do." Nor does it
seem to me that most theologians really believe that they
do, in their most self-transparent moments. But there
is a kind of unexamined tradition about "what Christian

theology is obligated to be," in which everyone by gentleman's agreement continues to follow certain rules about being "biblical" and "christocentric" without admitting that this is neither necessary, desirable, nor what really goes on in their reflections.

It is precisely modern historical investigation, Schweitzer believed, which demands of theology greater honesty and independence concerning its relationship to Jesus. If theology is not to remain simply archaic it must free itself from the hopeless notion that it has somehow to justify or explain away every word this remarkable first-century Jew uttered, every act he performed, and the ancient mythological framework and terminology within which he operated. Schweitzer himself seems definitely to have seen the data of theology—the "permanent" or "eternal" element to be distilled out of its historical containers—in the reality of a transcendent spiritual-ethical dimension, force, or will which is disclosed in a decisive way through Jesus but expresses itself in fresh forms in every new and never fully anticipated human generation. As he wrote in *The Quest of the Historical Jesus:*

Jesus means something to our world because a mighty spiritual force streams forth from Him and flows through our time also. This fact can neither be shaken nor confirmed by any historical discovery. It is the solid foundation of Christianity.[29]

Such an approach appears to me to offer the most viable way forward for Christian theology.

This is a laudable age of theological honesty. But theologians need to become still more explicitly honest about both their presuppositions and their methods, before one another, the church, and the world. The theologian's key doctrine still seems to be "justification by history," which few sincerely can or ought to believe any more and even fewer practice. I believe that Schweitzer, in his theory if not always in his practice, still thunders at us through the corridors of the twentieth century to stop playing theological games with Christianity's historical source; to shake the uncreative incubus of tradition and openly establish a creative relationship with the past; and thereby to become both intellectually and spiritually free.

III. Creation ex nihilo: Paradox or Contradiction?

The Christian doctrine of creation *ex nihilo* ("out of nothing") is not simply a paradox to human understanding; upon close examination it turns out to be flatly self-contradictory. According to *The Shorter Oxford English Dictionary*, a paradox is "a statement *seemingly* self-contradictory or absurd, though possibly well-founded or essentially true." [1] A self-contradiction is "a statement which contains elements that contradict [i.e., are logically inconsistent with] one another." [2] Creation "out of nothing" does not merely seem to be self-contradictory; it is so, and no amount of talk about "mystery" will relieve the contradiction. This is true not only of the doctrine's classical formulations but also of its contemporary restatements. The theological affirmations about the relation of God to the created order which "creation out of nothing" has sought to safeguard need to be dealt with in some alternative way. This important doctrine of classical Christianity is a matter of sheer credulity rather than faith.

In his contemporary study of the doctrine of creation,

Maker of Heaven and Earth, Langdon Gilkey writes: "With regard to the fundamental relation of God to the world, almost the entire tradition of Christian thought is in substantial agreement. . . . The variety . . . lies on the surface, in the differing philosophical tools each theologian employed to organize his thought. . . . This central theological idea that runs consistently throughout Christian history . . . is the doctrine of *creatio ex nihilo.*" [3] We may use Thomas Aquinas as a clear and influential example of the doctrine in its classical form. He defines "creation" in what he, along with previous Christian theology, understands to be its unique biblical sense when applied to God: " 'In the beginning God created the heaven and the earth.' To create is to bring a thing into existence without any previous material at all to work on." [4] Elsewhere Thomas states that "he is almighty, and he has no need for material to work on. One being alone proceeds from him, he, who is his equal, is the Son; all other lesser beings issue from his will, not his nature." [5]

The following propositions expressing the doctrine of creation "out of nothing" can be derived from Thomas' formulation:

1. God creates freely, by an act of "will," not out of necessity.
2. Created being is no part of the divine nature.
3. But neither is created being the product of material coeternal with God and independent of his will.
4. All created being—matter and form, flesh and spirit, everything other than God himself—is totally dependent for its existence and continuance upon the free action of God.

Proposition 1 excludes all forms of emanationism,

as for example in Hinduism and Neoplatonism. As a matter of fact, for most Christian theologians the natural emanation of finite being from the infinite cannot properly be called "creation" at all. Central to traditional Christian thought is the ontological difference between the Creator God and his creatures.

Proposition 2 excludes monism or pantheism. This exclusion must be seen together with emanationism in Proposition 1, since most forms of pantheism or monism involve an emanationistic view of the relation between infinite and finite. The second proposition emphasizes that *creatio ex nihilo* means that absolutely nothing but God is divine or has any claim to divinity. Nature, for example, is not an aspect of God; the human soul is not a "spark of divinity." The doctrine of creation "out of nothing" radically "de-divinizes" the universe, laying the philosophical groundwork, according to some theologians and historians, for the rise and dominance of scientific investigation and technology in Western culture.

Proposition 3 excludes any sort of dualistic cosmology, as in Plato's *Timaeus*. There the deity is a "demiurge," an architect molding cosmos (order) out of primordial chaos rather than a creator. For traditional and most contemporary Christian doctrine dualism puts the created order partly outside God's creative power and governance.

Proposition 4 summarizes the doctrine of creation "out of nothing." Absolutely everything that is not God is totally dependent for both its origin and preservation upon the free creative activity of God. "Everything that is not God" means the totality of finite being, physical and spiritual.

Let us now state the dilemma of *creatio ex nihilo*

in terms of its full implications: God is the sole ground of all finite beings. It makes no difference here whether this absolute priority is simply ontological, as in the view taken by some Christian thinkers that God eternally creates; or also "temporal," as in the more usual view that God begins creating at a point "in (or with) time." The crucial thing for both versions of creation "out of nothing" is that there is no "material" coexisting with or within God out of which to create a finite realm. There is not even a dialectical "nothingness" "over against" him which might serve as an opposite pole and limiting agent for the emanation of finite being out of his being. Ontologically speaking, the being of God equals being. Furthermore, there is absolutely no necessity in the divine creativity. God creates, not by "nature" but by "grace," not by necessary causation but out of "freedom." Yet God comes up with beings other than himself, *which are no part of his being.*

To be sure, classical Christian theology has affirmed the *analogia entis,* the *analogy* of being between the Creator and his creatures. But as Thomas says, it is the analogy of effects to their cause; it expresses the "imprint" of God in what he creates. Analogy is neither identity (univocity) nor total dissimilarity (equivocity). *Analogia entis* affirms a likeness between the being of creatures and the being of their Creator by virtue of their being effects of their creative cause. It scrupulously avoids identifying finite being with infinite being, or positing a continuum between them, in any way.

Here, then, is the dilemma:

1. There is no source of being except the being of God.

2. Finite being which is not the being of God exists. The question is: Do 1 and 2 constitute (a) a meaningful

paradox or (b) an irreconcilable contradiction? Christian theology traditionally and to a large degree at the present time answers with (a), but utterly and completely fails to shed any light on why they are a paradox and not a flat contradiction. This is in distinct contrast to theological development with regard to such central doctrines as the Incarnation and the Trinity. Much modern theology has done a creative job of interpreting the person of Christ and the unity-in-diversity of God in such a way as to show that if in the last analysis they are inexhaustible mysteries transcending reason, human reflection can at least partially illuminate them in ways which do not violently defy reason. The skeptic may not be convinced, but at least he can get some sort of grasp, in a sort of "as if" manner, on faith's "inner logic" expressed in Incarnation and Trinity. It is decidedly otherwise with creation *ex nihilo,* where we find much modern theology simply stating in new ways what classical theology had always unconvincingly said. The contrast between such theological progress in some areas and such arrested development in this one leads us to suspect that the reason lies in the genuinely self-contradictory and therefore unrescuable character of creation "out of nothing."

Twentieth-century Protestant theology has by and large been content merely to affirm that *creatio ex nihilo* points symbolically to the conviction that creation is totally dependent upon, but not identical or continuous with, God. Little attempt has been made to deal with the problem of the "nothing" in "out of nothing"; it tends to be glossed over by being informally regarded as a negatively symbolic way of expressing the mystery of finite being's total dependence upon, but nonidentity with, the being of God.

According to Emil Brunner, "the truth that God is the One who determines all things and is determined by none, is the precise meaning of the idea of Creation as *creatio ex nihilo*." [6] The doctrine, he goes on to say, "expresses something which is utterly beyond all human understanding. What *we* know as creation is never *creatio ex nihilo*, it is always the shaping of some given material." [7] Brunner resolves all difficulties by his appeal to revelation, but has the forthrightness to see the doctrine for what it is from a human standpoint: "We can only speak of Creation on the basis of Revelation. From our point of view as human beings, on the basis of our own intellectual efforts, *to speak of 'Creation' is . . . nonsense. . . .*" [8] The question that must be addressed to Brunner at this point is: Is the hiatus between human reason and divine revelation so great that the doctrine of creation is sheer "nonsense" and must simply be accepted as such? Is not believing what one's mind finds to be blatant "nonsense" credulity rather than faith? To be sure, faith transcends understanding; but is it obligated to contradict it?

The great philosophical theologian Paul Tillich, who might be expected to be keenly aware of the difficulties, ends up hedging on the issue of creation *ex nihilo*. He insists that the doctrine points to something which must be affirmed by Christianity: "The doctrine of *creatio ex nihilo* is Christianity's protection against any type of ultimate dualism. That which concerns man ultimately can only be that on which he ultimately depends." [9] Tillich maintains that the doctrine of creation points to two basic truths: "The first is that the tragic character of existence is not rooted in the creative ground of being; consequently, it does not belong to the essential nature of things. . . . The second truth . . . is that there is an element of nonbeing in creatureliness; this gives insight into the natural necessity of death and into the potentiality but not necessity of the tragic." [10]

It is all very well to talk about what the doctrine of creation *ex nihilo* "protects" or "preserves" or "points to" or "symbolizes," and Tillich, as in so many other areas, does this exceedingly well. But all this sort of talk does not relieve theology of the demand at the most basic level for sense rather than nonsense. It is right at this point, in trying to discuss what "creation out of nothing" could possibly mean in some coherent sense, that Tillich hedges:

> Now "nothing" can mean two things. It can mean the absolute negation of being (*ouk on*), or it can mean the relative negation of being (*me on*). If *ex nihilo* meant the latter, it would be a restatement of the Greek doctrine of matter and form against which it is directed. If *ex nihilo* meant the absolute negation of being, it could not be the origin of the creature. Nevertheless, the term *ex nihilo* says something fundamentally important about the creature, namely, that it must take over what might be called "the heritage of nonbeing." [11]

In this remarkable statement, Tillich says that the "nothing" in "out of nothing" can mean two things, and we are properly to infer that he means "only two things" since if there were a third alternative he would have mentioned it. Then he goes on to say that "nothing" in the Christian doctrine of creation cannot mean either one of the only two possibilities he sees, relative or absolute negation of being. But nevertheless, he concludes, Christianity needs to continue to affirm creation *ex nihilo*. The reader who is not committed in advance to the classical doctrine might well find it puzzling that, having failed to make any sense of an idea, the theologian does not draw the reasonable conclusion that perhaps something is wrong with the idea. Tillich, like many other contemporary theologians, was willing to revise and even reject classical Christian doctrine at certain other points for the sake of what he believed to be the truth; why the continued insistence on one of the least comprehensible doctrines of all?

Brunner, Tillich, and other twentieth-century theologians who have retained the doctrine of creation "out of nothing" as essential to Christianity have of course allowed its rationally self-contradictory character to be overruled by what they believe the doctrine protects or symbolizes in the Christian understanding of the relationship between God and the created order—chiefly the unqualified affirmation of the goodness of all created things. It virtually never seems to occur to most theologians that they might explore alternative ways to make such affirmations which do not depend upon a self-contradictory notion. Their failure to consider other possibilities, their offhanded and frequently ignorant rejection of the well-argued alternatives which certain thinkers have given us, their dogged repetition of the same old affirmations and denials—all this adds up to one of the most remarkable blind spots to be found in the otherwise liberated theologies of the twentieth century. The most extraordinary thing of all is that the biblical source, which continues to be important to contemporary theologians, affirms the goodness of the created order without a doctrine of creation *ex nihilo*! But of this more later.

Langdon Gilkey, who might be expected to have mined

the whole problem of creation *ex nihilo* rather exhaustively, simply states that at the heart of creation "out of nothing" is the concept of absolute origination: "Creation means primarily to bring process or finitude, in all its aspects, form and matter alike, into being out of nothingness. The movement of creation is not from unformed matter to formed object [as in Platonic dualism], but from the nonexistent to the existent. . . . Creation is the divine evocation into existence, out of nothingness, of finite being in its totality." [12] Gilkey nowhere stares squarely in the face and discusses the tremendous problems such an idea presents. He is content to assert: "The basic formula 'out of nothing' is in fact an explicit abandonment of any 'how' explanation. . . . By this paradoxical formula Christian thought has expressed its conviction that with regard to 'how,' the divine creation lies beyond our understanding." [13] Such a statement does not say nearly enough. Gilkey does not consider whether the idea is paradoxical or simply contradictory. He does not distinguish between lying "beyond our understanding" and lying squarely against it.

For most contemporary theological restatement, as for classical theology, *creatio ex nihilo* remains the Absolute Miracle. It differs in kind, and not merely in degree, from other miracles. According to classical theology, a miracle is an astonishing rearrangement within the natural order by the higher order of God. In other words, other miracles are transformations of what exists by a higher order of existence. The skeptic may well reject the reality of miracle, but at least the concept has a rationale within its framework of presuppositions. It can be argued for with some clarity and reason, even though it is believed to point to a mystery. But the Absolute Miracle of creation stands entirely outside all possible reference and reasoning.

In his excellent book *Issues in Science and Religion,* Professor Ian Barbour of Carleton College discusses at some length the implications of modern evolutionary theory for theological affirmations about the relation between God and the universe. As a Christian theologian as well as a scholar trained in the sciences, Professor Barbour is eager to bring about a creative synthesis of evolutionary theory and the Christian perspective on reality. The scientific picture of a universe and an earth in dynamic evolutionary process suggests to him the necessity for Christianity to emphasize the doctrine of God's "continuing creation," divine creative activity at work in the continual emergence of the universe.

In dealing with the idea of continuing creation theologically, Professor Barbour turns first to the biblical sources of the Christian view of God and the world. Examination of the biblical material on the relationship between God and the created order in the light of recent biblical scholarship suggests to him an affirmation and a denial. The affirmation is that "continuing creation is a biblical idea." "Almost every chapter of the Old Testament," Barbour continues, "witnesses to the conviction of God's *continuing* sovereignty over history and nature (the events of the Exodus, *ca.* 1300 B.C., are the paradigm), whereas there are relatively few references to primeval beginnings—and these are usually in late writings (Genesis 1 was written around 500 B.C.)." [14] The denial is extremely significant for our topic: "Creation 'out of nothing' is not a biblical concept."

Most scholars hold that it is not stated or implied in the biblical narrative. At the opening of the Genesis story there is a primeval sea, a background of darkness and chaos. The church historian Pelikan shows that the idea of *ex nihilo* was developed post-biblically as a defense of the goodness of the world and the absolute sovereignty of God against Gnostic ideas regarding matter as evil or as the product of an inferior deity. "So began the identification of creation primarily or exclusively with *creatio ex nihilo* which crowded continuing creation out of the attention of theologians." [15]

Like most other contemporary theologians, Barbour wants in some fundamental way to square his reflections with the biblical roots of the faith. Unlike most other contemporary theologians, he denies that creation "out of nothing" is an essential implication of the biblical material on God and the world. In fact, he is concerned to reject this traditional concept, particularly insofar as it entails God's temporal priority over his creation as well as his priority in status, as incompatible with the view of the universe which we have from the biological, geological, and physical sciences.

In his own brief positive reappraisal of the Christian doctrine of creation, Barbour draws upon the process philosophy of Alfred North Whitehead to suggest the following:

If, as we have proposed, the doctrines of creation and providence are combined in a concept of continuing creation, we do not have to abandon the idea of *dependence on God,* which both doctrines have traditionally affirmed. We may have to give up *creatio ex nihilo* as an initial act of absolute origination, but God's priority in status can be maintained apart from priority in time. We can even preserve some of the classical intent of *ex nihilo* by saying that novelty is as such not traceable to its antecedents. Each human being, for example, is truly a new creation, and every poem, painting, or symphony is a novel event which cannot be completely accounted for by its past. Creation is not just the rearrangement of the given, but the origination of the genuinely new. *Yet creativity always works in what exists to bring into being what did not exist.*[16]

Interestingly enough, Barbour's only concern with *creatio ex nihilo* is what he considers to be its probable incompatibility with the scientific picture of a universe in continual emergence; like most theologians, nowhere does he seem to find its logically self-contradictory character to be a problem. Furthermore, Barbour does not appear to be aware that to retain the view that God is the ultimate ground of reality but to reject creation "out of nothing" entails a *dualistic* perspective: i.e., God always has material on which to work which is dependent upon him but not "willed" or brought into existence by him. The last sentence of the above quotation clearly suggests that this is what Barbour intends to say. Having previously and approvingly pointed out what are in fact the dualistic tendencies of the creation story in Genesis 1, he also fails to see their upshot for theological cosmology.

Barbour's inability to entertain what I have called the dualistic perspective even though the logic of his position leads in that direction is well-nigh universal among theologians. Because of our usual theological training, the term "dualism" almost always means certain standard things to theologians—usually views such as Manichaeism or Zoroastrianism, which they do well to reject. The dualism of Plato in the *Timaeus* is also mentioned but always dismissed out of hand as somehow miles apart from the "biblical and Christian view." The "internal dualism" of a sophisticated modern thinker (and Christian believer!) like Edgar Sheffield Brightman of Boston University, for whom there are factors eternally within the divine experience which God did not create but which are subordinate to ("dependent upon") him, is almost universally ignored and not infrequently unheard of. Yet Brightman's view of the relation of God to the evolutionary process is in some respects strikingly close to a "mainstream" thinker like Barbour.[17]

Significantly, Professor Barbour combines his rejection of *creatio ex nihilo* with the retention of divine omnipotence, and the combination will not work. Omnipotence and creation *ex nihilo* are indissolubly linked; each implies the other. If one goes, the other logically goes too. A God who is always and intrinsically limited by something other than his own nature is not the almighty Creator of classical doctrine. A God who is truly omnipotent in the intended traditional sense is the God who freely creates beings other than himself which are not simply emanations of himself. In creating, God limits himself; but the limitations are self-imposed, not intrinsic.

But Professor Barbour goes on making the familiar theological moves, continuing to affirm the divine omnipotence, maintaining God's voluntary self-limitation in the activity of creating, and ritually distinguishing this view from Plato's approach in the *Timaeus*.[18] Yet so far as I can see, what he says in rejecting creation "out of nothing" and what he says in affirming divine omnipotence are simply contradictory. In the one case God always has "material" (limitations other than self-imposed ones) to work on; in the other case God's only limitations are self-imposed.

The significance of Professor Barbour's rejection of *creatio ex nihilo*, however, cannot be underestimated. Here is a first-rate scholar who wants to stand squarely within the "majority" Christian theological tradition who finds himself driven to question the suitability of the doctrine both on biblical grounds and in the light of modern evolutionary theory. It is precisely the fact that in other respects he does not wish to stray from familiar theological affirmations (e.g., divine omnipotence and the rejection of dualism) that makes his concession so important. It is beside the point that he does not question creation "out of nothing" on what I consider to be the prior grounds of its being a self-contradictory concept. The crucial thing is simply that Barbour is clear and impressive evidence of a mainstream contemporary Christian scholar who believes that Christianity can reject creation *ex nihilo* and lose nothing thereby.

It is worth going back briefly to Professor Barbour's contention that the concept of creation "out of nothing" is not a biblical idea. He cites several Old Testament scholars past and present in support of this view, including S. R. Driver, H. Wheeler Robinson, and Edmond Jacob. A recent example of the concurrence of Old Testament scholarship on this interpretation of the creation story in Genesis 1 is Professor John H. Marks's commentary on the book of Genesis in *The Interpreter's One-Volume Commentary on the Bible*. He writes of the opening verses of chapter one:

Creation begins when God imposes order on primeval, non-personal chaos by calling **light** into existence. This P account has obvious parallels in the Babylonian creation and flood epics (cf. also Pss. 74:13-15; 89:10; Isa. 51:9). It seems to picture a chaotic storm churning over the primordial dark and mysterious abyss of infinite and formless water. Out from this God summons order, thus creating the universe (cf. Job 26:10-14; Pss. 29:10; 93:3-4; 104:5-9). Time begins with that creation. Nothing is said of the origin of the chaos or of God's activity prior to creation (cf. Ps. 90:2). The question about whether creation is out of nothing (*creatio ex nihilo*) is also irrelevant to the story. God's creation **in the beginning** is unique and inexplicable, and appropriately the Hebrew word *bara,* here translated "create," is applied in the OT only to God's activity (see below on vss. 20-23, 24-30; 2:2-4*a;* cf. Isa. 40:26, 28; 45:18). An ordered universe is conceivable only as a divine act of creation.[19]

Notice that in this *locus classicus* of the doctrine of creation, "creation" equals imposing order on primeval chaos: "Out from this [chaos] God summons order, *thus creating the universe.*" The divine creative activity *even on these terms* is considered unique by the P writer and entitled to the singular designation *bara,* because it is only *God* who in his power and sovereignty and eternity is able to subdue the primordial chaos and mold it to his creative purposes. The created order remains dependent upon God, except only in the sense of deriving its being from the will of God.

The creation story in Genesis 1 thus has more similarities with Plato's myth of creation in the *Timaeus* than most theologians are still willing to admit. The differences are matters of degree rather than kind. Plato writes: "Desiring, then, that all things should be good and, so far as might be, nothing imperfect, the god [the Demiurge] took over all that is visible—not at rest, but in discordant and unordered motion—and brought it from disorder into order, since he judged that order was in every way the better." [20] The fundamental and important difference between Plato's account and the Genesis story is that Plato's Demiurge designs the created order according to the rational pattern of eternal Ideas, Forms, or Universals which constitute the true realm of being. In other words, the

Demiurge refers to something "outside" himself for his standard in creating. By contrast, for the Genesis account and biblical faith generally, God refers to nothing outside himself, apart from his own wisdom, in creating; in Platonic terms, the eternal Ideas are within the mind of God himself. Thus the biblical account ascribes greater ultimacy and sovereignty to God than Plato does to the Demiurge. But both stories agree in viewing "creation" as fashioning cosmos (order) out of chaos, *not* bringing something into being out of nothing. And that means a dualistic perspective on God's creative activity, not the view expressed in creation *ex nihilo*.

Influenced too heavily by classical tradition, many theologians persist in refusing to see that to interpret the relationship between God and the created order dualistically does not intrinsically require the sacrifice of divine sovereignty, creaturely dependence, or the goodness of the created order. (It also resolves the impossible dilemma of divine omnipotence and the problem of evil, but that is another topic.) To be sure, it does require some revision in these traditional Christian affirmations, but not the sort of revision which jeopardizes their substance. As we have seen, there is no doubt in the Genesis creation myth of God's sovereignty over man and the created order. The primordial chaos is subject to the divine lordship, and it is God alone who fashions it into an ordered universe. In the modern philosophical dualism of Brightman, those uncreated factors which roughly correspond to the primordial chaos in Genesis are eternally within and dependent upon the divine experience, although not the result of the divine will. Thus they are always under the divine sovereignty, although not in the sense of deriving their existence from

God's creative fiat. The lordship of God is his sovereignty as ultimate context of reality and as shaper and purpose-giver of the cosmos.[21]

As for the goodness of the created order, the same Genesis story which sees God as sovereign molder rather than omnipotent creator *ex nihilo* also declares that the work of creation was "very good" (vs. 31). The work of creation, it will be recalled, is on the view of the P writer the activity of bringing order out of chaos, of imprinting whatever purpose and direction and rationality the universe possesses. On this view we may say that the created order is good insofar as it manifests this divine ordering and purposing. There is no necessary threat within a dualistic perspective such as this one that matter will be singled out and labeled evil, as in the Manichaean nightmares of theologians. *All* things—matter and spirit, body and soul—are good insofar as they express the creative activity of God in purposefully shaping order out of chaos. Nor does that other dualistic bogey man of theology appear in principle within this sort of dualistic framework—evil as an ultimate constituent of the universe, as in Zoroastrianism. The factors eternally given to the divine experience with which God has to work are not in themselves evil or good, but simply neutral. The "primordial chaos" or, to use Brightman's term, "the Given," contains the potentialities for both good and evil. As Brightman says, whatever realities are coeternal with God are "both instruments and obstacles" to his will. [22] They provide both the stuff out of which the only good we know is made, and also the intractabilities which resist and thwart God's loving purpose and produce what we call evil. But in and of themselves they are properly to be thought of as neutral.

It is true that in the Old Testament the myth of the primeval chaos, like the corresponding myths of Israel's Near Eastern neighbors, has negative connotations, and evil is sometimes interpreted in the biblical writings as a lapse back into chaos.[23] Clearly, a divinely ordered and directed cosmos is infinitely preferable to a chaos of senselessness and confusion. But my point is that even this old mythical view of creation had to recognize, if its adherents reflected on the matter, that it is precisely the original chaos which furnishes the raw material transformed by God into cosmos. It is the chaotic state of things when God begins to create, not things themselves, which is by comparison with creation undesirable. God's unique and powerful creative activity lies in "beating back" this chaotic state of affairs and bringing order out of it. As Professor Marks comments on the conclusion of the Genesis 1 story, in which creation is declared "very good": "The chaos has been effectively restrained, and order prevails. . . ." [24]

To be sure, speaking of the created order as "good" in the dualistic way I have sketched represents a revision in the classical view of the goodness of creation undergirded by "creation out of nothing." On that view all things are intrinsically good because they derive not only their form and purpose but also their existence totally from God. But the clearly dominant theological concern in clinging to this view has been to guard against perspectives on God and the world which would call aspects of creation intrinsically evil (e.g., matter) or remove any aspect of reality from God's sovereign and loving care. I have argued, however, that a dualistic outlook by no means necessarily entails either of these theological nemeses. It does demand relinquishing the notion of the fundamental existential dependence of the created order upon God's sheer willing; but that does not seem to me to be too high a price to pay for being able to speak coherently instead of incoherently, and nothing that I can see of the significant positive affirmations which Christianity wants to protect is lost.

I have dwelt at some length on an informal exploration of what I have called a dualistic alternative to *creatio ex nihilo* which finds mythical expression in the first chapter of Genesis and philosophical expression in the writings of a modern thinker like Edgar S. Brightman, as an example of some viable possibilities which most theologians have not bothered to examine. Christianity does not stand or fall with the self-contradictory doctrine of "creation out of nothing," and I have sought to present one alternative which relates both to the biblical sources and to modern thought simply by way of showing that there are ways of dealing with the problem of creation which demand neither the sacrifice of what is essential to the Christian message nor the sacrifice of the intellect. Some may find even the dualistic perspective on the relation of God to the universe a bit too speculative for their tastes, and prefer more modest views which limit themselves to religious experience of God as presence to man or transcendent dimension within reality and remain "agnostic" about his relation to the total scheme of things. But I recognize that the sort of dualism I have presented comes closest to fulfilling the cosmic-speculative demands classically expressed in the doctrine of creation "out of nothing," and therefore I have offered it as the perspective which would require the least radical shift of Christian cosmological thinking.

In this essay I have argued that the classical and still widely held Christian doctrine of creation "out of nothing" is not, as its defenders claim, simply a mysterious paradox but an inescapable self-contradiction. To assert both that there is no source of being except the being of God and that finite being which is not the being of God exists is to contradict oneself. To demand adherence to this self-contradiction is credulity, not faith; it is to run squarely counter to reason and not simply to transcend it.

I have given examples of leading twentieth-century theologians who have continued tenaciously to cling to *creatio ex nihilo,* out of an unexamined assumption that it protects certain Christian affirmations about the relation of God to the universe which cannot be protected in any other way. In challenging this view I have presented the dissenting arguments of an otherwise mainstream contemporary Christian thinker, Professor Ian Barbour, who rejects creation "out of nothing" both on biblical grounds and on the basis of the modern scientific evolutionary picture of the universe. Professor Barbour's inconsistent clinging to the doctrine of divine omnipotence, which is inseparable from the idea of *ex nihilo,* simply reinforces the importance of his rejection of creation "out of nothing" as a thinker who is by no means a theological maverick.

Finally, I have suggested that the rejection of the doctrine of creation *ex nihilo* coupled with the retention of the view that God is the ultimate context of reality, such as we find in the thought of Barbour, points in the direction of a dualistic perspective: i.e., a view which holds that the "material" of creation is coeternal with God and does not depend upon him for its existence but rather for its form and direction, although it may lie entirely within the divine experience. I have pointed out that according to contemporary biblical scholarship, the myth of creation in Genesis 1 is closer to dualism, such as we find in Plato, than to the traditional doctrine of *creatio ex nihilo*. I have argued that a sophisticated dualism such as we find in the writings of Edgar Sheffield Brightman preserves all that is essential in the Christian affirmations of the divine sovereignty and the goodness of the created order which the traditional doctrine was chiefly concerned to protect.

In an age of theological openness to knowledge and rational considerations which have brought about sweeping revisions in many aspects of Christian thought, there can be no good reason why Christian thinkers should cling to nonsensical ideas, however venerable, in certain areas. The tired and stereotyped rejections out of hand of alternative positions on the matter of creation simply represent a deeply worn rut into which theologians continue to get themselves. It is time for some completely fresh thinking on the doctrine of creation in the light of reason, modern scientific knowledge, and some discrimination of what is essential and what is nonessential in Christianity. Happily, some exciting and fruitful thinking is going on,[25] but a great deal more needs to be done.

IV. The Dilemma of Omnipotent Love

A brief essay by British philosopher Antony Flew which opened the "Theology and Falsification" symposium in the *University* journal twenty-one years ago raised a disturbing old question in a new way. Flew's essay, together with responses by Richard Hare and Basil Mitchell and a rebuttal by Flew, was reprinted in the landmark volume *New Essays in Philosophical Theology*,[1] and has been reproduced in several books of readings in the philosophy of religion since that time.

Flew's argument runs like this: Theological statements are intended by their users to be assertions, and not merely (to use John Wisdom's phrase) "picture preferences" or (to cite Flew's own list of alternatives) "crypto-commands, expressions of wishes, disguised ejaculations, [or] concealed ethics." [2] Now "to assert that such and such is the case is necessarily equivalent to denying that such and such is not the case." An assertion is genuine if it is falsifiable; that is, if we can state the conditions in experience which would render it false. Flew then goes on to observe that "it often seems to people who are not religious as if there was no conceivable event or series of events the occurrence of which would be admitted by sophisticated religious people to be a sufficient reason for conceding 'There wasn't a God after all' or 'God does not really love us then.'" [3] Flew uses the illustration of a child dying of inoperable cancer of the throat whose earthly father is frantic in his efforts to help but whose heavenly Father remains silent. Confronted with such an occurrence, the spectacle of innocent suffering, the religionist will "qualify" what the love of God means to render it compatible with this ostensibly falsifying occurrence. If pressed further, he will qualify it further, until the statement "God loves us" turns out to be compatible with any and every conceivable state of affairs, no matter how horrible. But this is to empty what started out to be an assertion of any claim to be a genuine assertion. It dies, Flew maintains, "the death by a thousand qualifications." [4] If "God loves us" is compatible with any conceivable kind or amount of evil, does it not turn out to be vacuous and uninformative?

Flew concludes by posing to Christian theism the question: "What would have to occur or to have occurred to constitute for you a disproof of the love of, or of the existence of, God?" [5] His question, in theological terms, is essentially an inquiry concerning the problem of evil, traditionally one of the most difficult problems for Christianity and one of the greatest stumbling blocks to the non-Christian.

The child dying of inoperable cancer of the throat always recalls to me a memorable scene in Albert Camus's novel *The Plague,* the ghastly and agonizing death of the mayor's son from bubonic plague. *The Plague* is probably the clearest and most moving expression of Camus's own humanism and his rejection of Christianity. For Camus the spectacle of human suffering from both natural causes and the oppression of other men was always the insurmountable stumbling block. An omnipotent God who would create and allow to continue such a world, and in addition forever sanctify such suffering by disclosing himself supremely in a tortured and crucified man, Camus considered cruelly unjust and not loving. His rejection of God was intensely moral: the gods in their powerful silence are capricious and unjust; when man acts capriciously and unjustly he denies his common humanity and becomes like the gods.

In *The Plague* Dr. Rieux and Father Paneloux are together with the child and watch his last dreadful agonies. Rieux is an agnostic physician who devotes himself to ministering to human affliction in a no-nonsense way, knowing that death wins in the end but believing that we have an obligation to one another in the meantime as fellow exiles in the same boat to alleviate suffering and injustice. He more than anyone else in the novel is the spokesman for Camus's own views. Father Paneloux is a learned Roman Catholic priest, portrayed by no means unsympathetically by Camus, who is the spokesman for what Camus believes to be the main Christian approaches to evil. As the two men leave the bedside of the dead boy, the exhausted Rieux turns on Father Paneloux and says sharply:

"Ah! That child, anyhow, was innocent, and you know it as well as I do!..."
"Why was there that anger in your voice just now? What we'd been seeing was as unbearable to me as it was to you."
Rieux turned toward Paneloux.
"I know. I'm sorry. But weariness is a kind of madness.

And there are times when the only feeling I have is one of mad revolt."

"I understand," Paneloux said in a low voice. "That sort of thing is revolting because it passes our human understanding. But perhaps we should love what we cannot understand."

Rieux straightened up slowly. He gazed at Paneloux, summoning to his gaze all the strength and fervor he could muster against his weariness. Then he shook his head.

"No, Father, I've a very different idea of love. And until my dying day I shall refuse to love a scheme of things in which children are put to torture." [6]

This scene expressing Camus's religious skepticism is appropriate in the present context. Flew, too, thinks he has "a very different idea of love" from that of the Christian when he speaks of the love of God in the face of the unspeakable suffering of children. He asks indirectly if there is any relationship whatsoever between human love and the love of God when the Christian seems willing to qualify the word "love" beyond all familiar recognition in speaking of God.

Of the two responses to Flew's challenge in that part of the "Theology and Falsification" discussion which appears in *New Essays,* it is the essay by Basil Mitchell that leads into the crux of the matter. Mitchell agrees with Flew that statements about God are intended to be real assertions about the nature of reality. He points out, however, that they constitute a rather special type of assertion: they are falsifiable, but not conclusively. The reason they are genuinely but not ultimately falsifiable, says Mitchell, is to be found in the basis or ground upon which faith rests, and in the nature of faith itself.

Mitchell constructs a parable about a member of the resistance movement in an occupied country during wartime, who meets a stranger. They talk at some length.

The stranger assures the partisan that he is on the side of the resistance, and urges him to trust him no matter what happens. The partisan is deeply impressed by the stranger and trusts him. After that the stranger is seen sometimes helping the resistance, and sometimes seeming to be on the side of the enemy. The partisan is grateful in the former cases and does not allow the latter cases to destroy his trust, although they constitute for him a severe trial. Sometimes the partisan asks the stranger for help and gets it; sometimes he does not. He is committed to trusting the stranger on the basis of his initial encounter with him, but the stranger's ambiguous behavior does indeed count agonizingly against his trust. Mitchell raises the question of how long the partisan can maintain his position without its becoming ridiculous, and replies:

> I don't think one can say in advance. It will depend on the nature of the impression created by the Stranger in the first place. It will depend, too, on the manner in which he takes the Stranger's behaviour. If he blandly dismisses it as of no consequence, as having no bearing upon his belief, it will be assumed that he is thoughtless or insane. And it quite obviously won't do for him to say easily, "Oh, when used of the Stranger the phrase 'is on our side' *means* ambiguous behaviour of this sort." In that case he would be like the religious man who says blandly of a terrible disaster, "It is God's will." No, he will only be regarded as sane and reasonable in his belief, if he experiences in himself the full force of the conflict.[7]

What Mitchell is arguing is that for the Christian the fact of evil *does* "count against" the assertion that "God loves us"—but not conclusively, because of the existence of another set of facts and their interpretation. Faith embraces both a "because of" and an "in spite of," and it is just the full dialectic of this which Mitchell believes that Flew oversimplifies. The Christian believes that there are sufficient grounds in his experience for trusting in the reality and love of God: specifically, the historical events culminating in the ministry, death, and victory over death of Jesus as recorded and interpreted by the biblical witnesses and appropriated personally by those who become incorporated into the Christian community. The Christian clearly believes "because of" specific things which have happened in human experience; his faith does not float free of the earth. In terms of Mitchell's parable, the partisan trusts the stranger because of his impression of the stranger.

But just as there are some experiences "because of" which the believer trusts in God and his love for man, so there are other experiences which for the believer agonizingly "count against" the divine reality and love. He trusts "in spite of" these other experiences. Amid the perplexity of the human condition, he gives the weight to what he sees embodied supremely in Christ and reflected in all manifestations of truth, beauty, and goodness, and trusts that in the wisdom and compassion of God there is an ultimate explanation and meaning to the dark side of things which is now hidden from us. Flew seems to want theistic statements, says Mitchell, to be "provisional hypotheses to be discarded if experience tells against them." They are instead "significant articles of faith," he replies, for which certain confirming experiences sufficiently outweigh the disconfirming experiences of evil.[8]

But all is not over yet in the "Theology and Falsification" discussion—indeed, just now do we come to the crux of the matter. In his closing rebuttal Flew reveals for the first time what he regards as the heart of the problem of evil for the theist: the belief that God is not only infinitely loving but also omnipotent and omniscient. The theist's difficulty, Flew argues,

is that he has given God attributes which rule out all possible saving explanations. . . . Suppose the Stranger is God. We cannot say that he would like to help but cannot: God is omnipotent. We cannot say that he would help if only he knew: God is omniscient. We cannot say that he is not responsible for the wickedness of others: God creates those others. Indeed an omnipotent, omniscient God must be an accessory before (and during) the fact to every human misdeed; as well as being responsible for every non-moral defect in the universe.[9]

In another important essay in *New Essays,* "Divine Omnipotence and Human Freedom," Flew focuses specifically on the omnipotence of God in relation to the Christian doctrine of creation: "What the doctrine of creation means is that all power is from God, that all things and creatures are always and utterly dependent on God, for their beginning and preservation, in and for their powers, their activities, and their limitations." [10] According to Flew, "The only picture which begins to do justice to this situation is. . . that of the Great Hypnotist with all his creatures acting out, usually unknowingly, his commands. To fail to appreciate this is to fail to take the theological doctrine of creation seriously."

To the standard theological rejoinder that God voluntarily limits his power in creating a universe other than himself, Flew replies that "if the limitation is real it must involve that the Universe is now to that extent out of control, and contains things independent of God; which is precisely what the doctrine of creation denies." [11] Flew concludes that "the whole notion of an omnipotent creator God is logically vicious. If this is so the problem of evil cannot arise, since the notions of God as either all-powerful, or all-good or as even existing at all will all be equally vicious. This is a position to which the present writer is very much inclined...." [12]

The traditional Christian doctrine of creation, classically expressed in the idea of *creatio ex nihilo*—creation "out of nothing"—does indeed assert that everything other than God is totally dependent for its existence and nature upon the omnipotent will of God. According to Flew, there is no possible way on these terms to absolve God of ultimate responsibility for the world's evil.

Flew is correct, I would argue, in his general assessment of the logic of omnipotence, even if he is mistaken on one or two internal points which I will consider presently. I want to suggest that the insistence by Christianity on the all-powerfulness of God, together with its corollary creation *ex nihilo*, is perhaps the fundamental Achilles heel of the faith. It is certainly not necessary that a religion "solve" the problem of evil in some airtight manner; to make such a demand is perhaps to ask the impossible. But the doctrine of divine omnipotence not only does not offer even a partial solution to the problem; it exacerbates it to the point where faith becomes a commitment which flies absurdly in the face of hard experience and God becomes a monstrosity. In what follows I will try to show that the standard and even the best defenses of divine omnipotence fail; that unless Christian theology is willing to abandon the almightiness of God, the falsifiability case must go to the humanist hands down.

1. The Classical Doctrine

To turn first to the biblical literature for the roots of the doctrine of omnipotence: The Hebraic mind, it is well known, was notoriously unspeculative in its thinking. The leading ideas about God, for example, which form the center of classical Christian doctrine appear in highly concrete, "existential" form in the biblical writings and are only developed in their philosophical implications during the centuries of Christian contact with the Greek heritage of rational inquiry.

The divine Reality who the prophets of Israel believed disclosed himself in the life and history of their people came among them with power as well as with grace and judgment. Yahweh who had liberated Israel out of serfdom in Egypt, who guided the destiny of the Hebrews, was a transcendent Power who in time came to be seen as sovereign Lord over all peoples and history, and in fact as sovereign over the entire creation, "visible and invisible."

But even in the loftiest reaches of the biblical understanding of God, as in Second Isaiah (Isa. 40–55) and the New Testament, the references to his attributes always remain concretely oriented to the human situation and resolutely unspeculative. The biblical writers speak of God's "almightiness" in just this existentially dominated, imprecise way. We find in the biblical literature virtually no reflection whatsoever on the problem of "omnipotence." The central conviction is that God is sovereign Lord over man's life and destiny. By religiously compelling and coherent extension this mysterious and powerful God is seen as the ultimate context of, and power behind, all of reality. Beyond that the Hebraic mind does not venture.

So the New Testament writers can speak in the same breath of God's "almightiness" on the one hand, and on the other of its many obvious limitations: human freedom and deep-rooted sinfulness, the Satanic rebellion which is now even seen as having the world temporarily in its control, disease, and death. The "Good News" of the New Testament is the story of the sovereign God's struggle, in the person of Christ, against the powers of Satan, sin, and death, and his triumphantly and conclusively defeating them through Jesus' death and resurrection—a drama of real conflict with real obstacles to the divine lordship. All this appears side by side with no apparent awareness of the "problem of omnipotence," precisely because the biblical literature remains within the realm of the existential, of religious experience, and has no interest in pushing things to what later Christian theologians have considered (mistakenly, as I hope to show) their "logical conclusion" or "clear implications."

The doctrine of the sovereign power of God, then, arises out of what faith believed it experienced as the concrete actualities of historical events, not out of speculation about divine possibilities. In its attempts to wed biblical revelation and the Greek philosophical ideas first of Plato and then of Aristotle, classical Christianity formulated the theological concept of omnipotence. Theologians and Christian philosophers tended at times to become preoccupied with the kinds of questions the philosophical mind is inclined to ask about omnipotence: Can God do what is logically contradictory? Does the divine almightiness transcend even the moral commandments God has revealed to man? Do the omnipotence and the infinite love of God entail that this universe is "the best of all possible worlds"?

First the Protestant Reformers, and latterly recent theology both Protestant and Roman Catholic, have sought to recover the dynamic and nonspeculative character of the faith originally expressed in the biblical literature. Criticism and redefinition of traditional theological ideas have characterized nineteenth- and twentieth-century theology to a unique degree, influenced as it has been by such phenomena as the development of historical research on the biblical writings and the rapid advance of knowledge in the natural and social sciences. Key themes in contemporary Protestant and Roman Catholic thought have included the recovery of the biblical literature as living historical witness and the use of existentialist analyses, with their dynamic, concrete, and largely unspeculative descriptions of human experience. Common to all this has been a radical rejection or modification of much of the Greek-inherited metaphysical apparatus which had dominated much traditional Christian theology.

However, it is striking that despite these changes most contemporary theology continues to affirm the doctrine of divine omnipotence and agrees with classical theology in the basic outlines of the defense of God's almightiness in the face of the world's evil. That defense centers in the concept of *divine self-limitation*. All proponents of the doctrine of divine omnipotence have begun from this position, demanded as it is by the biblical testimony to the obvious restrictions on God's power. There are indeed limitations on God's total power, they point out—the creation of a universe other than himself, human and angelic freedom with the Satanic rebellion and sin which have resulted—and the defense of his almightiness in the face of evil rests upon these limitations. But for a theistic absolutism the only limits to God's power are *self*-limitations; he is not limited by anything other than himself.

The divine self-limitations are seen to be of two sorts: (1) those arising from the nature of God himself, and (2) those which are "decisions" of God, free acts of his will.

For most Christian theology, God is limited in the sense that he cannot do what is contrary to his nature. Perhaps the two chief examples of such essential self-limitation are God's goodness and his truth. God is goodness itself; therefore it is impossible that he do what is evil. The divine wisdom is truth itself, the source and standard of the rational structures of the universe and the laws of human reason. Thus God cannot do what is logically self-contradictory or destructive of rational structure. He may and does do what transcends the categories of finite human reason, but not what contradicts them. So God, on this view, is not capricious. He is self-limited to the extent that he cannot defy his own moral and rational nature. God cannot suddenly make what he has called evil henceforth good, nor can he make A to be not-A.

The second class of self-limitation on God is the voluntary acts of his free will. These are the most interesting and the most crucial for the issue of divine omnipotence and the reality of evil. According to "mainline" Christian theology, God voluntarily limits or "contracts" his power by creating beings other than himself. It is of course distinctive of the traditional Christian view of creation that, although God does not create out of pre-existing "material" (like the Demiurge in Plato's *Timaeus*), nevertheless the being of creatures is not the being of God. This is precisely what *creatio ex nihilo* expresses: God creates beings whose being is not divine, yet without employing anything other than the "fiat" (let it be) of his own creative will. The created order is not a "natural" emanation out of the divine being, as in Neoplatonism and Hinduism. Nor is it the work of a divine architect imposing order (cosmos) on a material chaos which co-exists with him, as in Plato and John Stuart Mill. God voluntarily limits himself by willing to create "out of nothing" beings which are genuinely other than himself although ultimately dependent for their being and continued existence upon his all-powerful will.

Within the created order Christian theology distinguishes two types of beings which represent different sorts of divine self-limitation: (1) the things that comprise what we usually call "nature"—animals, plants, minerals, planets, stars—which behave in regularly patterned ways but apparently lack freedom of choice; and (2) "moral-spiritual" beings—man, perhaps some forms of life in other solar systems and galaxies, and, traditionally, beings (angels, both good and evil) who transcend the spatio-temporal order. These beings are all characterized by at least some degree of freedom to choose between good and evil, to make of themselves what they will be.

The voluntary self-limitation of God in the natural order has usually been mapped out under some such rubric as the distinction between "primary" and "secondary" causes. God is the primary cause of nature: he brings it into being and it is always totally dependent upon God for its continued existence. But as part of his rational organization of the universe God has "built into" it a system of natural causation ("secondary" causes) which operates in a subordinately autonomous way. So, for example, although in a primary or ultimate sense the walnut tree outside my study window is caused by God in the sense of fundamental ontological dependence, he causes it to be brought into existence and to have the characteristics it has by "indirect" means, i.e., through the system of natural causes whose explanation is part of the work of the natural sciences. Thus the tree is caused both by God and by the germinating of a certain kind of seed in the soil, which was produced by another tree, which . . . , and so on backwards and ever wider through the evolutionary process of life on this planet to the formation of the universe.

In traditional theology God "suspends" or "interferes with" this order of secondary causality in what are called miracles. But these are explained, not as contradictions of the rational working of nature, but as expressions of the fuller rationality of nature's Source. Many contemporary theologians have abandoned this older defense of miracles and returned to what they consider to have been the original, biblical emphasis, in which a miracle is understood primarily as a sign to faith of the activity of God in the world and human life which may or may not be scientifically inexplicable. In both cases, however, God is seen as able to exercise his power as he wills even within the relative autonomy of natural processes.

The second form of voluntary self-limitation by God is the creation of beings with an even higher degree of autonomy than nature, the freedom to make choices, thereby at least partially determining their own destiny in a manner which is not reducible to natural processes. As contemporary theologians are fond of saying, human history and culture are the unique product and realm of what Tillich calls man's "finite freedom." Man clearly participates in natural processes and dwells within the natural environment as a product of animal evolution. But he also transcends these processes in free decision as a moral-spiritual being, thereby emulating in a finite way (the "image of God") his infinite Creator. In the Bible and traditional theology there are also thought to be purely spiritual beings—angels—who are likewise endowed with freedom. Since they do not labor under the natural limitations of man, their freedom has a wider scope.

For most Christian theology, God does not override human freedom. He is always present to man, acting in various ways to disclose himself and call man to himself, but he does not coerce. On its best face the doctrine of hell is a kind of extreme expression of God's respect for human freedom: he permits us to turn away from him, to alienate ourselves from him everlastingly, without interfering. Similarly with the angels, such as Satan, who according to Bible and tradition has eternally alienated himself from God by his own choice. Human and angelic freedom is the severest self-limitation on the part of the omnipotent God.

The all-powerful God has willed to limit himself in these ways, Christian tradition has said, out of his wisdom and love. For some reason which to us is not always readily apparent, God chose to create this sort of universe and not some other; these sorts of creatures (men and angels) to have the opportunity of everlasting union with him and not some others. It is a universe which at least in a subordinate way "runs itself" by the laws and causal processes which God has given it. Human beings are creatures possessing a still higher autonomy, that of relative self-determination through free decisions, including the determination to turn away from God and good and choose evil. In his

109

omniscience, before which "a thousand years are but as yesterday," God has known throughout eternity what course the natural order and moral-spiritual beings would take and what interventions in it he would make and not make; but he has regarded everything as in the long run "worth it" to the end he has in view.

What, then, of the problem of evil on this view of divine self-limitation? Natural or nonmoral evil is the unfortunate by-product of what is essentially good: a rational, stable natural order. It is precisely the combination of the relative autonomy of "secondary causes" and the law-abiding regularity of nature which sometimes produces occurrences which affect human beings in ways that are evil. Tornadoes, for example, with which my own part of the United States is familiar, result from the confluence of certain air masses that are part of a general climatic pattern which usually functions in a beneficent or at least not destructive way. Disease-producing microbes are living organisms thrown up by the, on the whole, humanly appreciated variety of evolutionary forms, and are matched by beneficial microbes which support life. The particular stable structure of this universe, embodied in natural causality, makes life and science possible at all. This structure and causality sometimes bring together occurrences and processes which produce intense suffering or colossal disaster for human beings; but this is the price to be paid for an autonomous and orderly universe.

The evil committed by moral-spiritual beings (moral evil) is on the view of theistic absolutism the result of the autonomy of freedom over against God. This probably accounts for the greatest number of the things man calls evil: tyranny, cruelty, prejudice, hatred, injustice, indifference, greed, power-worship, etc. The biblical and classical-theological symbol of Satan expresses the belief that there is a primordial misuse of freedom even among purely spiritual beings (angels) before the creation of man. There is a force of evil in the created order which is extremely powerful and cosmic in scope, contributing to the moral evil of man through its malevolent influence.

But let us concentrate on moral evil at the human level. As in the case of purely spiritual beings, God regards the relative autonomy of finite freedom as such a great good that he is willing to allow that autonomy to take its course even though it results in much evil. In the case of human beings, unlike angels, the particular forms which evil choices take are determined in part by our status as bodily, earthly creatures in a spatio-temporal environment. So, for example, excessive power is an evil to which both angels and men are tempted, but only among men does it take such forms as political control over geographical territory; while presumably sexual incontinence is a sin possible only to man.

In the elucidation of moral evil classical Christianity has brought in very centrally the doctrines of the fall of man and original sin. They have been interpreted variously, especially in modern theology, but basically they are symbols pointing to and attempting to account for what appears to be man's universal predisposition to choose evil more than good, to turn selfishly in upon himself rather than selflessly toward God and his fellowmen. The relevant aspect of the doctrines for our purposes is that, despite this greater tendency to evil, man is neither absolved of responsibility for his plight nor deprived of his freedom to turn toward the good. To be sure, his freedom is seen as vitiated, but by no

111

means is it impotent. While salvation comes only by the grace of God, God offers to all men his saving grace and the choice is man's to accept or reject.

Very significantly, what this theological defense reveals is a sound instinct trying to support a wrong conclusion. The sound instinct, based upon our real experience of the world and our common sense about the qualities that make a being worthy of worship, is the recognition that there are important limitations—even obstacles and resistances—to the power of God. The wrong conclusion is that God is nevertheless infinitely powerful.

2. Objections

Let us turn now to objections to the "self-limitation" defense of divine omnipotence, first considering Flew's criticism. It will be recalled that according to Flew, "if the limitation is real it must involve that the Universe is now to that extent out of control, and contains things independent of God; which is precisely what the doctrine of creation denies." Flew is incorrect in stating things this way, although his objection points to a substantial criticism of the "self-limitation" defense.

We have seen that at the heart of the theological defense is the distinction between the ontological dependence of the created order upon the Creator and its relative independence or autonomy in terms of operation, whether the regular causal process of the natural order or the "finite freedom" of the moral order. Flew seemingly does not accept this distinction, although he does not tell us why. However, I fail to see what is wrong with it. I see no insuperable difficulty in maintaining that the being of all things is continually dependent upon the being of God while allowing the details of their relationships among one another within this ontological framework to be autonomously produced. To be sure, God is believed to involve himself in the details of the created order in specific ways— for example, miracles and his active presence among persons—but he does so as another factor or element within the patterned network of causes and the environment of moral influences. I am supported in this positive assessment of the distinction by Professor John Hick of the University of Birmingham in England, an able philosopher within the British analytical movement as well as a first rate historical and creative theologian who has offered what I consider to be the strongest defense of the indefensible case for divine omnipotence. Hick says of the distinction between proximate autonomy and ultimate dependence:

God has created this universe, in so far as its creation relates to man, as a neutral sphere in which his creatures are endowed with a sufficient degree of autonomy to be able to enter into a freely accepted relationship with their Maker. From this point of view, God maintains a certain distance from man, a certain margin for a creaturely independence which although always relative and conditioned, is nevertheless adequate for man's existence as a responsible personal being. This "distance" is epistemic, rather than spatial. It consists in the circumstance that God, not being inescapably evident to the human mind, is known only by means of an uncompelled response of faith. . . . This circumstance requires that man's environment have the kind of autonomy which, in fact, we find it to have. The environment must constitute a working system capable of being investigated indefinitely without the investigator being driven to postulate God as an element within it or behind it. From the point of

113

view of this conception of God, the autonomy of nature, as it is increasingly confirmed by the sciences, offers no contradiction to religious faith. The sciences are exploring a universe which is divinely created and sustained, but which has its own God-given autonomy and integrity.[13]

When Flew, therefore, says that insofar as God limits his power by creating, "the Universe is now to that extent out of control and contains things independent of God," the theological answer must be "Yes and No." Yes, the created order is "out of (God's) control" and "independent" to the extent that it enjoys the relative autonomy of "secondary causation," stable "laws," and finite freedom. No, it is not "out of control" and "independent" insofar as it depends every moment for its continued existence upon the creative power of God and operates within a total ontological framework of divine purpose. The doctrine of creation, *pace* Flew, does indeed deny absolute but not relative or secondary creaturely independence. Flew's rejection of the "self-limitation" defense, then, is too hasty and oversimplified.

But I said that Flew's inadequate remarks point to a substantial criticism—indeed, to *the* substantial criticism—of the "self-limitation" defense of God's almightiness. What the Christian doctrine of creation "out of nothing" *does* deny is that any limitation on God's power proceeds from anything but his own nature or will. And that remains the fatal flaw in the defense of divine omnipotence which prevents it from overcoming Flew's humanistic objections. The whole trouble with the "self-limitation" defense is precisely the "self": All limitations upon God are *self*-imposed and therefore entirely his responsibility.

God limits himself by creating natural and moral-spiritual beings other than himself, an order of things the basic character as well as the material of which is his work. There is no pre-existing "matter" or chaos or opposing power of evil to impede or limit God's design. He has a *carte blanche* in creating, holding absolutely all power and being and bringing other realities into being by sheer fiat. Furthermore, he is absolutely wise and good. Thus God willed to bring into existence *this particular* created order, knowing throughout eternity how it would unfold in its subordinately autonomous way—including its human "fall," its medieval Black Death, its Pakistan tidal wave, its Auschwitz. Relatively autonomous, yes; but the specific nature of this autonomous creation is directly the work of God, while its particular development is from the beginning within his eternal purview. Christian theology cannot finally escape saying that while God does not directly will the Black Death or original sin or Auschwitz, he designs the created order in a way which yields these possibilities and furthermore knows that the possibilities will be actualized. My conclusion must be that if the only limitations upon God are self-limitations, then God does not escape ultimate responsibility for the particular kind of created order we have with its share of natural and moral evil.

The tenacity of the doctrine of divine omnipotence even among contemporary theologians, and the almost off-handed way in which they decisively reject (not really argue against) suggestions that God is finite as to power and go on bravely but futilely trying to reconcile the divine omnipotence with the sometimes staggering evil in the world, is puzzling. What is extraordinary about this stubbornness is that in virtually all other areas modern Protestant theologians, at least, have been cheerfully willing to update and sometimes radically to revise the Christian faith.

Nowadays, for example, it is conceded on many sides that Jesus was limited in his knowledge to his time and place. Indeed, a number of theologians proclaim him the Incarnation of God while granting that he was flatly mistaken about a crucial aspect of that around which his whole ministry revolved: he believed that the kingdom of God which he was inaugurating would come in its fullness very soon, bringing about the end of history. A few Protestant thinkers are even willing to judge Jesus' moral perspicacity defective on occasion! [14] The virgin birth and the bodily resurrection, of course, "went" for many theologians long ago. Miracles, which I mentioned earlier, are often redefined in such a way as to remove them from conflict with natural causation. Nor do most contemporary Protestant theologians seriously entertain the possibility that there are evil spirits inhabiting the world, causing mental and physical illness. With Protestant neo-orthodoxy, Satan underwent a certain rehabilitation, but present-day Satanology is often presented in such an abstract guise (as in Tillich's "demonic structures of reality") as to be almost unrecognizable.

I do not list the above theological revisions by way of saying, as orthodox Christian apologist C. S. Lewis and a surprising number of skeptics as well are too often prone to say: "Contemporary theology has given away the Christian faith or reduced it to 'Christianity-and-water.' Back to classical Christianity, which at least has richness and backbone." [15] Far from it. Surely the theologian must be guided by intellectual honesty as well as faith, and many—by no means all—find themselves driven by their loyalty to truth to make all or some of the revisions I have listed as examples.

My purpose is simply to show how much ground modern Protestant theology has been willing to give in other seemingly vital areas for the sake of truth. Why, then, does there persist this determination to hold to the divine omnipotence in the face of all odds? Let us look at some prominent examples from modern theology of thinkers who continue to affirm God's almightiness and creation "out of nothing."

3. Contemporary Defenses of Divine Omnipotence

Those theologians, both Protestant and Roman Catholic, who still wish to maintain and defend the doctrine of God's all-powerfulness, do so by returning to the concrete, unspeculative categories of the biblical approach and criticizing the philosophical tendencies of classical theology's handling of the doctrine. So Karl Barth, for example, rejects speculation about God's power as "power in itself" and "whether God can bring it about that twice two equals five," as unbiblical and unchristian. Barth looks instead to the actuality of the power revealed in Christ: "This power, God, is the power of His free love in Jesus Christ, activated and revealed in Him. . . . What in His grace God is and effects is the essence of all that is called ability, freedom and possibility." [16] But at the same time, "There is no reality which does not rest upon Him as its possibility, no possibility, no basis of reality, which could limit Him or be a hindrance to Him. He is able to do what He wills." [17]

117

In *The Christian Doctrine of God,* Emil Brunner is greatly concerned to counter the philosophical tendency of classical theology to speculate about omnipotence in terms of divine "Being" and *potestas absoluta,* with the original biblical understanding. He writes that "the power that God possesses—in contrast to the abstract idea that 'He can do everything'—always means exercising power over *something.*" [18] Brunner dwells on the biblical notion of God's self-limitation: "God *limits Himself* by creating something 'over against' Himself, which He endows with a relative independence." Nevertheless, "it is God Himself who creates this limitation —hence He is also free to remove it." "This idea of Omnipotence . . . means that this self-limitation of God, because it is the act of His own will, does not erect any barrier to His power or His authority." [19] God's "power cannot be limited by anything or anyone" except himself.[20]

Even Rudolf Bultmann, with his thoroughgoing existentializing of theological assertions and radical criticism of the biblical sources, lapses on occasion and interprets "faith in God the Creator" in this way: "God's creation is a creation out of nothing; and to be God's creature means absolutely and in every present to have one's source in him, in such a way that were he to withhold his creative will the creature would fall back into nothing." [21]

Representative of post-Vatican II Roman Catholic thought is the well-known and controversial "Dutch Catechism" (in English: *A New Catechism*), said to be largely the work of the distinguished theologian Edmund Schillebeeckx. The discussion throughout is permeated by a reliance on biblical and personalistic categories and a sitting lightly to speculation which ventures beyond this living, dynamic framework of thought. Thus in the *Catechism's* affirmation of God's almightiness:

The whole of revelation asserts most emphatically that evil does not stem from a dark power which is as primordial and as potent as God. . . . No, God, in whom there is no darkness, is the one origin of all things. But then the question of where evil comes from becomes still more awkward. If its source is not to be sought in some eternal force of evil, is its origin then God—and how can that be, since he is the eternal goodness? The whole of scriptural revelation attests that God is not the cause of evil but its antagonist. At the same time, the Bible teaches us where to look for the primary cause of wickedness and suffering: in the freedom of the free creature which corrupts its own goodness. . . .

How do we know that the infinitely omnipotent God is omnipotent precisely in the manner which we have thought out? Perhaps his omnipotence is more incomprehensible, more marvellous—more omnipotent—than man can realize.[22]

Like the discussions in Barth, Brunner, and Bultmann, the *Dutch Catechism*, with its otherwise admirable use of concrete terminology, simply sidesteps the implications of omnipotence and relegates the matter to a mystery and a paradox which mortal vision cannot penetrate. But this evasion will not do. To be sure, the nature of God and his relation to the created order are in the final analysis "mysteries," in the sense of matters which are (1) in principle never simply accessible to empirical knowledge and its development, and (2) inexhaustibly open rather than soluble like a problem. But it is one thing reverently to acknowledge mystery, and another simply to refuse to follow the logic of the clear affirmations one *has* made. If God is omnipotent he does not escape final responsibility for what he has

119

created; no resort to mystery will get him off this particular hook. As for paradox, I take it that a paradox is a proposition which seems to be self-contradictory but in fact is not. Unless the ideas of God and the divine love are to be totally removed from any relationship to human understanding and placed in an obscure and lofty realm inaccessible to human comprehension, it is not paradoxical but self-contradictory to say that God is omnipotent but not responsible for the world's evil.

John Hick, who is otherwise a decidedly liberal theologian,[23] has constructed what I consider to be the strongest case for divine omnipotence in the face of evil which we have. A look at his argument will summarize what has been said thus far.

Hick rejects straightaway the alternative of conceiving of God as finite in power: "To solve the problem of evil by means of the theory (sponsored, for example, by the Boston 'Personalist' School) of a finite deity who does the best he can with a material, intractable and coeternal with himself, is to have abandoned the basic premise of Hebrew-Christian monotheism; for the theory amounts to rejecting belief in the infinity and sovereignty of God." [24] Hick footnotes his mention of the Boston "Personalist" School of philosophy with a reference to its most distinguished representative, Edgar Sheffield Brightman. Brightman, a Christian himself, offered in his writings the most sustained argument for the finitude of God's power which we have. (I should add that by no means did all the Boston Personalists agree with him here; most, in fact, held to the traditional position of omnipotence.) It is unfortunate that Hick, in the manner typical of defenders of divine omnipotence, does not bother to describe and argue against Brightman's position but merely asserts that it "amounts to rejecting belief in the infinity and sovereignty of God." This statement as a description of Brightman's position is simply incorrect.

Professor Hick goes on to say that

any theory which would avoid the problem of the origin of evil by depicting it as an ultimate constituent of the universe, coordinate with good, has been repudiated in advance by the classic Christian teaching . . . that evil represents the going wrong of something which in itself is good. . . . Whatever exists is, as such, and in its proper place, good; evil is essentially parasitic upon good, being disorder and perversion in a fundamentally good creation. This understanding of evil as something negative means that it is not willed and created by God; but it does not mean (as some have supposed) that evil is unreal and can be disregarded.[25]

Two preliminary remarks are worth making about this passage. The first is that it is difficult to see how a theory which depicts evil as an ultimate constituent of the universe "avoids" the problem of the origin of evil any more than the classical Christian theory based upon divine omnipotence. Indeed, a case can be made for saying that a theory which forthrightly concludes that evil is somehow "built into" reality along with good, genuinely tries to find a solution, however we may judge its success; while a theology based upon divine omnipotence is prohibited *a priori* from speaking meaningfully of the origin of evil. But the second point is that Brightman's theory, which is what Hick still seems to have in mind, does *not* depict evil as an ultimate constituent of the universe in the sense Hick intends. According to Brightman, "All theistic finitists agree that there is something in the universe not created by

God and not a result of voluntary divine self-limitation, which God finds as *either obstacle or instrument* to his will." [26] That which is "given" to the divine experience is *both* limitation *and* opportunity; it is the "raw material" which contains both the intractabilities which result in evil and the embodiment of all that we know as good. It would be more accurate to say that this "raw material," not evil per se, is an ultimate constituent of the universe on Brightman's view. This is a crucially important distinction in light of what Hick has to say in justification of belief in the almightiness of God.

Let us turn, then, to the main point—Hick's defense of divine omnipotence. He reveals what is the nerve of the theological defense, although its logical steps need spelling out: the Judaeo-Christian belief that the whole created order is "the creation of a good God for a good purpose." Here is the answer to our "Why?" question about the tenacity of the doctrine of divine omnipotence. What is at stake for Christian theology is the fear that if we allow that anything created is not totally dependent upon God for its matter as well as its form, its existence as well as its nature, then we cut the nerve of the affirmation of the goodness of the created order. We have historical examples, such as Manichaeism, of religions which trace evil to matter as its root and regard only "spirit" as good. Manichaean tendencies are well-nigh universal in all religions, including popular Christianity (as in soul/body dualism). There are other forms of religious dualism which place some aspect of the created order outside the pole of the creative activity of divine goodness, but the Manichaean is perhaps the most popular and pervasive. The Christian theologian vigorously continues to believe that a fundamental aspect of the divine self-disclosure to Israel and in Christ is the essential goodness of all things created—angels, man, and nature—and that such dualistic tendencies are wrongheaded.

The logic of the goodness of the created order goes something like this: God is good; therefore what he creates is good. God is omnipotent; therefore absolutely everything other than God is entirely created by and dependent upon his will (creation *ex nihilo*). Taking this information, we form the proposition:

What God creates is good.

God has created everything other than himself.

Therefore everything other than God is good.

There can be simply no denying the religious and moral power of this idea. The belief that all creatures *qua* creatures—body as well as spirit, nature as well as man—are good is a world-affirming and life-reverencing doctrine. One can only lament that Christianity has not clung to the religious and moral implications of this product of its Hebraic roots as clearly and firmly as it should have. But religious and moral significance is one thing and the question of truth is another; and here is where the problem lies. The price a Christian theology which clings to divine omnipotence pays for its affirmation of created goodness is too high, since God does not avoid being responsible for the evil in the created order—however it proximately arises and however much it is viewed as simply the distortion of what is essentially good—as well as the good. Furthermore, paying this price is unnecessary. It by no means follows that the only alternative to the doctrine of God's all-powerfulness is a view which denies God's sovereignty and sees some aspects of the created order as inherently evil. A kind of obstinate blind spot on this matter consistently leads theologians to think that the only alternatives are A and B and to neglect the possibility of C altogether.

In his own original and thoughtful statement of Christian theodicy, Hick rejects the "majority report" theodicy classically propounded by Augustine—with its familiar account of an originally perfect creation from which man by his free choice fell (and with him the universe) into sin, suffering, and perdition—as historically, logically, and morally incredible. He finds more satisfactory the "minority" tradition given its original expression in the writings of the second-century theologian Irenaeus. "Following hints from St. Paul," Hick writes, "Irenaeus taught that man has been made as a person in the image of God but has not yet been brought as a free and responsible agent into the finite likeness of God, which is revealed in Christ. Our world, with all its rough edges, is the sphere in which this second and harder stage of the creative process is taking place." [27]

God has designed the created order, then, not as a paradise which man turns into a mess, but as an evolutionary process yielding an environment in which man may develop through obstacles and challenges into a mature moral-spiritual being destined to enjoy eternal growth and fellowship in God. Hick describes his position this way:

It would seem, then, that an environment intended to make possible the growth in free beings of the finest characteristics of personal life, must have a good deal in common with our present world. It must operate according to general and dependable laws; and it must involve real dangers, difficulties, problems, obstacles, and possibilities of pain, failure, sorrow, frustration, and defeat. If it did not contain the particular trials and perils which—subtracting man's own very considerable contribution—our world contains, it would have to contain others instead.

To realize this is not, by any means, to be in possession of a detailed theodicy. It is to understand that this world, with all its "heartaches and the thousand natural shocks that flesh is heir to," an environment so manifestly not designed for the maximization of human pleasure and the minimization of human pain, may be rather well adapted to the quite different purpose of "soul-making." [28]

Yet Professor Hick has the peculiar virtue among contemporary theologians of recognizing clearsightedly that a doctrine of life after death is absolutely necessary to any "justification of the ways of God to men"—particularly a theodicy which insists upon divine omnipotence:

But if we look at this world in this way, as a place of soul-making, we cannot avoid noticing how extremely ambiguous it is and how utterly uncertain its success. Sometimes indeed obstacles breed strength of character, dangers evoke courage and unselfishness, and calamities produce patience and moral steadfastness. But sometimes they lead instead to resentment, fear, grasping selfishness and tragic disintegration of character. Life can be soul-destroying as well as soul-making. And therefore this type of theodicy, which finds its clue to the meaning of evil in God's eventual decisive bringing of good out of it, is driven to look beyond this world and to take seriously the Christian hope of eternal life. This aspect of Christianity tends to be soft-pedalled nowadays, presumably because it makes such an openly transcendent claim. But no theodicy is possible without such a claim. For if human personality becomes extinct at the moment of bodily death then a great part of the evil of this world must remain forever unjustified. [29]

It should be added that Hick decisively rejects the Augustinian "majority" Christian belief in an everlasting hell. Only the ultimate redemption of all men is consistent with the purpose of a God who is both omnipotent and loving and has set us in the midst of the kind of universe we inhabit.[30]

Hick finally takes the bull unflinchingly by the horns and affirms that *God is indeed ultimately responsible for the created order* as we find it:

The . . . Irenaean type of theodicy has been more ready to say explicitly that God, as the sole Creator and Ruler of the universe, bears the ultimate responsibility for it. For there is no one else to share that final responsibility; and it is perhaps as presumptuous as it is ineffectual for theologians to attempt to relieve God of it by taking it upon mankind. But Christian faith adds that God, by whose design our way to final good lies through evil, and to final happiness through suffering, has himself in the person of Jesus the Christ shared fully our human suffering and our struggle against evil. He was Immanuel, which means "God with us," in the depths and darkness of human experience, leading us through resurrection, which is the birth of faith within us, to the fulfillment of our existence in the Kingdom of God.[31]

The "Irenaean theodicy" of John Hick seems to me to be the most reasonable resolution of the dilemma of divine omnipotence and the fact of evil in modern theology. But by admitting that God is ultimately responsible for the way things are he simply recognizes with refreshing but damning candor where the doctrine of omnipotence logically leads. By this admission Hick "gives the game away" completely.

So Hick simply has the merit of stating frankly and unequivocally what omnipotence is all about: God is ultimately responsible for everything. Hick's vision of the divine purpose is certainly morally preferable to most traditional Christian views: God ultimately brings all human beings into the joy of everlasting fellowship with himself. An eternity for all, of growth in grace, peace, happiness, and communion with other persons and God himself, is definitely more worthy of a loving, omnipotent God than the everlasting damnation of at least some portion of humanity.

But even on Hick's scheme we must ask, Why in the world would an all-powerful God of love deliberately design this long, slow process of evolution with its false starts and tremendous waste and the human condition as we have it with its large propensity to sin, its untold numbers of tortured, stunted, wasted lives, its gross inequalities, its distortions and oppressions—even for the sake of heaven? To put it another way: Does even eternal life justify all that the Black Death and Auschwitz symbolize? I recognize that it is quite possible to answer "Yes" to this question; Hick certainly seems to. There is always the old reply, for example, that we finite beings have only a limited perspective; we cannot see the whole picture as God can. If we could, we would understand the relation of what seems to be so much evil to the larger scheme of things.

But the analogical character of language about God seems to me to raise fundamental questions. How much evil can we allow an all-loving, omnipotent God to bear the responsibility for without equivocating over the word "love"? A loving person tries within the limits of his finite power and wisdom to create situations in which possibilities of growth and fulfillment are maximized. He seeks in all situations to alleviate suffering, to protest and try to overcome injustice. Now if God were infinite in love but finite in power, struggling against obstacles not of his own making, the analogy between a loving person and a loving God would be a strong one. But if God holds all power whatsoever and has deliberately set up the world order we have, then the analogy is weakened considerably and in fact ends up equivocating.

We have seen Antony Flew's charge that Christianity's insistence upon divine omnipotence makes its talk of divine love unfalsifiable and equivocal to be eminently justified. We have looked at the traditional defense of God's almightiness at its best and seen that if the only limitations upon God are self-limitations—as both classical and most contemporary theologians maintain —then God is finally responsible for natural and moral evil and cannot be called "loving" without considerable equivocation. We have examined what I consider to be the best defense of omnipotence, that of John Hick, and seen that it succeeds only by giving the game away and frankly admitting that God is indeed responsible for the state of the universe. Hick's espousal of universal salvation was seen to be the only reasonable conclusion on such a view, but one which fails to balance out all that God puts man through. These dilemmas lead to a consideration of whether there are alternative views of the relationship between God and the world which are compatible with what is essential to Christianity while avoiding the disastrous logic of omnipotence; but that is the subject of another essay.

V. Alternatives to Omnipotence

What are the alternatives to the traditional Christian view of the relationship between God and the world? There would seem to be four: monism, dualism, pluralism, and what for want of a better word I would call "existentialism."

The first alternative, religious monism, is that varied and important group of perspectives which share the conviction that there is one ultimate reality of which all other beings are emanations or manifestations, rather than creations in the "mainstream" Christian sense; but some explanatory remarks are in order. The two most significant and influential forms of religious monism are, first, Hindu thought in some of its most basic tendencies, especially as they were given their extreme and most consistent expression in the Advaita Vedanta (nondualistic interpretation of the Vedic writings) school of the great ninth-century Indian philosopher Shankara; and second, that late, intensely religious development of Platonic philosophy chiefly exemplified by the philosopher-mystic Plotinus (third century A.D.) and his school of thought called Neoplatonism.

Neoplatonic ideas had a profound influence on Christian thought between the fourth and the thirteenth centuries, significantly affecting Augustine (late fourth-early fifth centuries), "Dionysius the Areopagite" (fifth century), and John Scotus Erigena (ninth century). Most modern forms of monism, influenced usually by the great philosophers Spinoza (seventeenth century) and Hegel (nineteenth century) seem to me to be more philosophical than religious in character, although they have deeply influenced thinkers whose primary interests were religious.

I have not included monism in my discussion of alternatives to classical Christian theism for three reasons: In the first place, religious monistic systems share with "mainstream" Christian theism the view that all reality has its ultimate source in God alone, and therefore at the most basic level are faced with the problem of evil in a way which is at least formally similar to that of Christianity. In one way or another, God remains the omnipotent source of everything, and in this essay we are searching precisely for "alternatives to omnipotence." In the second place, religious monism is difficult to reconcile with some of the central tendencies of the biblical sources of Christianity. In those Christian thinkers who were greatly influenced by Neoplatonism, we see a profound tension and a drawing back at critical points in favor of biblical ideas. I am concerned to discuss "alternatives to omnipotence" which are likely to be regarded by Christians as more nearly consonant with the biblical roots of their faith. Thirdly, the problems and possibilities of monistic systems of religious thought are reasonably well known and written about, while dualism and pluralism are much less familiar or likely to be entertained as options. The third alternative I will discuss, "existentialism," is not unfamiliar, but it has not often been interpreted from the standpoint I am proposing.

1. Dualism

The next alternative to the prevailing Christian cosmology is a form of *dualism*. By "dualism" I mean the view that there is another reality co-ultimate with God which is neither a divine manifestation (monism) nor a divine creation (traditional Christian theology). Dualism is an example of what one of its chief modern exponents, Edgar Sheffield Brightman, called "theistic finitism"; that is, it considers that God is finite in power (although not necessarily in goodness or love) and thus decisively frees him of responsibility for the world's evil. As Brightman states, "A theistic finitist is one who holds that the eternal will of God faces given conditions which that will did not create, whether those conditions are ultimately within the personality of God or external to it." [1] Plato was an "external dualist," taking the view in the *Timaeus* that God or the "Demiurge" is confronted with chaotic material coexistent with and "alongside" himself out of which he shapes a cosmos but which always remains resistant to his will.[2] Brightman, on the other hand, was an "internal dualist," positing what he called "The Given"—the laws of reason and "brute fact"—eternally within the experience of the divine Self but not a result of the divine will.[3]

Brightman arrives philosophically at an idea of God as "personal consciousness of eternal duration; his consciousness is an eternally active will, which eternally finds and controls The Given within every moment of his eternal experience." [4] "The Given" to Brightman "consists of the eternal, uncreated laws of reason and also of equally eternal and uncreated processes of non-rational consciousness which exhibit all the ultimate qualities of sense objects (*qualia*), disorderly impulses and desires, such experiences as pain and suffering, the forms of space and time, and whatever in God is the source of surd evil." The Given "is eternal within the experience of God and hence had no other origin than God's eternal being"; but "it is not a product of will or created activity." [5]

The relationship between God and The Given is described by Brightman in the following manner:

God's will is eternally seeking new forms of embodiment of the good. . . . In this process, God, finding The Given as an inevitable ingredient, seeks to impose ever new combinations of given rational form on the given nonrational content. Thus The Given is, on the one hand, God's instrument for the expression of his aesthetic and moral purposes, and, on the other, an obstacle to their complete and perfect expression. God's control of The Given means that he never allows The Given to run wild, that he always subjects it to law and uses it, as far as possible, as an instrument for realizing the ideal good. Yet the divine control does not mean complete determination; for in some situations The Given, with its purposeless processes, constitutes so great an obstacle to divine willing that the utmost endeavors of God lead to a blind alley and temporary defeat. At this point, God's control means that no defeat or frustration is final; that the will of God, partially thwarted by obstacles in the chaotic Given, finds new avenues of advance, and forever moves on in the cosmic creation of new values.[6]

We can see here that for Brightman The Given is not evil per se; it is both instrument or raw material in the achievement of whatever good is achieved in the universe and obstacle to the good. Brightman also affirms the ultimate control of God over that which resists his will while rejecting the traditional Christian idea that he has absolute control.

Brightman deals with the doctrine of creation by arguing that although "the reality of the physical universe is located wholly within the conscious experience of God," [7] he "has to create as a will limited both by reason and by nonrational content." [8] In setting forth his view of creation, Brightman succinctly and sharply rejects divine omnipotence and its corollary creation *ex nihilo:*

> Creation means only that God is responsible for exercising redemptive love; it does not mean that he is either responsible for or acquiescent in the evils which his will does not create, but finds. If we hold to creation and regard it as the act of an unlimited will, there is no escape from Bowne's *obiter dictum* that the "world-ground, by its independent position, is the source of the finite and of all its determinations." On this basis, no rational solution of the problem of evil in creation is possible; one must take refuge in an almost blind faith. The hypothesis of a finite God makes a rational, open-eyed faith possible. [9]

One of the most devastating arguments against divine omnipotence, Brightman believed, is what we know of the evolutionary process: "Not only is there colossal waste in the life process; there is also what appears to be a great deal of unsuccessful experimentation." [10] At the same time, the movement of life can be seen as "a creative or emergent evolution," an emergence of the increasingly complex out of the simple, of life out of nonlife, of mind and value out of submental processes. "Thus," Brightman observes, "the evidence of evolution

133

is seemingly contradictory. It points toward purposeless waste and futility; and it points toward purposeful creation and value." [11] In terms of a theistic view of the world, Brightman concludes:

> The hypothesis which these facts force on us is that of a finite God. Let us suppose a creative and rational will at work within limitations not of its own making. Then the world of life as we see it is what would be expected if the hypothesis is true; it appears to be the work of a spirit in difficulty, but a spirit never conquered by the difficulties. Particular purposes may be thwarted; the dinosaur and the heath hen may perish. Nevertheless, the general purpose of life and mind and value always finds new channels, new avenues of expression. It is never entirely dammed up. [12]

Brightman insists on the fact that theistic finitism—or dualism, as I have been calling it—makes much more sense of living religion than does the traditional belief in God's almightiness. "The divine control of that in the universe which the divine will did not create is a spectacle of suffering and victory—an eternal Calvary with an eternal Easter—which is fitted to elicit the profoundest religious emotions of reverence, gratitude, and faith." [13] He goes on to argue that belief in a finite God provides greater incentive to commitment to moral and social values, better grounds for belief in cosmic advance, and a more meaningful understanding of prayer.

Dualism has the great merit of preferring to worship value and goodness even if it means sacrificing some degree of power. It offers what is undoubtedly a theistic view of things which commends itself to Christian common sense and experience of the world more than the doctrine of omnipotence—a point to which I will return shortly. Here God genuinely struggles alongside us to overcome evils not of his own making; like us, he encounters genuine resistance and intractability in things which he did not arrange.

Interestingly and significantly, as Brightman observed, there is a profound discrepancy between Christianity as a living religion and the doctrine of omnipotence, a discrepancy reflected very much also in the writings of theologians. The existential power of Christianity as Good News to sinful man lies in the stirring drama of God's dynamic victory over sin and death in Christ. In Christ God is seen as disclosing himself decisively as *agapē*-love, sharing our lot, teaching and healing us, suffering our pains and dying our death. In this man Jesus, God is believed to wage a terrible struggle with the powerful forces of evil, supremely represented by Satan, and through Christ's life, death, and resurrection victoriously demonstrates that his love is more powerful. This is the message which is the life-blood of Christian worship, belief, and living. It is a message of concrete triumph and hope because it is the story of God struggling with and overcoming *genuine obstacles to his will.*

Now all this makes excellent religious sense within a framework other than that of divine omnipotence. We have the heroic and inspiriting picture of a divine ally and leader who works together with us to realize values out of the long, slow cosmic evolutionary process, who genuinely seems to struggle against forces not of his own devising. As C. S. Lewis, who certainly held to the doctrine of omnipotence, wrote in *Mere Christianity:* "I freely admit that real Christianity . . . goes much nearer to Dualism than people think. One of the things that surprised me when I first read the New Testament seriously was that it talked so much about a Dark Power in the universe. . . . Christianity agrees with Dualism

135

that this universe is at war." Of course, as Lewis points out, "The difference is that Christianity thinks this Dark Power was created by God. . . ." [14] (Lewis, of course, has in mind extreme forms of dualism such as Zoroastrianism, but his remarks apply to dualism generally.) And just there is where all the problems inherent in the logic of omnipotence begin flooding back in.

Whether it is possible to be confident that a God who is genuinely finite in power will surely triumph is a stock criticism but not an insuperable problem with ultimate dualism, as we have seen. In Brightman's scheme, "The Given" is within the divine experience and therefore remains subordinate to the reality of God. Certainly Christianity combines its practical dualism with a total confidence in the victory of God. But the full implications of omnipotence take the ultimate seriousness out of the whole protracted struggle against evil. For in the last analysis God alone has set up the conditions under which all this happens, and he knows throughout eternity what happens and how it all turns out. This is dangerously close to the Hindu view of the created order as *maya*, as the creative-destructive "play" or "sport" of God.

Christian theism tends to combine a practical dualism with an ultimate view of divine responsibility for everything, and the two simply will not hang together consistently. If Christian theology were fully dualistic it could avoid Anthony Flew's criticisms, at which we looked in the preceding essay, and make the case that its assertions about God are falsifiable. In fact, of course, as Flew points out, in terms of the traditional affirmation of omnipotence, Basil Mitchell's parable and his arguments lose their force. Mitchell's parable and discussion are in fact an appropriate statement of living Christianity, which is a practical dualism; it is only against the backdrop of divine omnipotence (which Mitchell espouses) that they fail to make sense.

Christian theology can abandon divine almightiness for dualism only by giving up also the doctrine of creation *ex nihilo,* with its affirmation that everything in all creation is the product of God's creative activity. Brightman, as we have seen, freely granted that "the theory of a finite God entails a view of creation different from that of traditional theism," [15] and rejected creation "out of nothing."

Most theologians continue doggedly to affirm omnipotence and *creatio ex nihilo,* with hardly even a scornful nod in the direction of coming to grips with the dualistic alternative. Even among theologians in the twentieth century, so open in other respects to fundamental revisions in Christian thinking, views such as Brightman's have been almost totally ignored or cold-shouldered as eccentric. This is unfortunate, since clinging to divine omnipotence renders divine love—which is after all the distinctive message and force of Christianity—highly dubious. I have dwelt at some length on the dualistic alternative, because its retention of the conviction that God is the ultimate reality grounding the universe probably renders it more nearly acceptable than the other two alternatives we will consider, for Christians used to thinking of God in cosmic terms.

2. Pluralism

The third possibility is *pluralism.* Religious pluralism is the view that God may not be the ultimate ground of

137

the universe, but simply one reality among many. The most intelligent and persuasive exponent of the pluralistic perspective was the distinguished American philosopher William James. James vigorously argued that a finite, struggling God coincided much better with the plain man's actual experience of the divine than the lofy Creator of heaven and earth. He referred to the pluralistic view as "piecemeal supernaturalism," and considered it much sounder intellectually than the rarefied, unifying abstractions of traditional theology and much philosophy. James called himself a "radical empiricist," basing his philosophical views on investigable experience but refusing to settle for reductionistic interpretations of experience especially at the human level. But as an empiricist, James refused to draw inferences from data which extended further than he believed to be inductively warranted.

In his classic study *The Varieties of Religious Experience*, James drew only those theological conclusions which he believed to be warranted by the actual data of religious experience. The result was a pluralistic view of the relation of God to the universe: "In the interests of intellectual clearness, I feel bound to say that religious experience, as we have studied it, cannot be cited as unequivocally supporting the infinitist belief. The only thing that it unequivocally testifies to is that we can experience union with *something* larger than ourselves and in that union find our greatest peace." [16] In a fuller statement James sets forth his own suggestions:

The practical needs and experiences of religion seem to me sufficiently met by the belief that beyond each man and in a fashion continuous with him there exists a larger power which is friendly to him and to his ideals. All that the facts require is that the power should be both other and larger than our conscious selves. Anything larger will do, if only it be large enough to trust for the next step. It need not be infinite, it need not be solarity. It might conceivably even be only a larger and more godlike self, of which the present self would then be but the mutilated expression, and the universe might conceivably be a collection of such selves, of different degrees of inclusiveness, with no absolute unity realized in it at all.[17]

In *A Pluralistic Universe* James wrote:

The line of least resistance, . . . as it seems to me, both in theology and in philosophy, is to accept, along with the super-human consciousness, the notion that it is not all-embracing, the notion, in other words, that there is a God, but that he is finite, either in power or in knowledge, or in both at once. These, I need hardly tell you, are the terms in which common men have usually carried on their active commerce with God. . . .[18]

As I have said, James believed it to be a fundamental principle in the search for truth not to infer more in the conclusion than is warranted by the premises. We have the fact of religious experience among human beings. As James persuasively argued in *The Varieties of Religious Experience* and elsewhere, a nonreductionistic account of the data must be open to the possibility that there is a real coefficient of religious experience which is not reducible either to the psyche or to the natural or social environment. James believed that the nature of religious experience, together with other data such as some of the findings of psychical research, made the reality of what human beings have called God or the divine not only possible but quite probable on "radically empirical" grounds. But if we are to be guided by the rules of inductive reasoning in this matter, he argued, we have no warrant without considerably more data than we have for inferring that the "superhuman consciousness" is the supreme reality behind the universe, as in monism and traditional Christian theology. Nor do we even have warrant for the assumption of dualism that there is another reality equally ultimate with God. We are entitled to infer only a reality sufficient to produce religious experience among human beings; in other words, the pluralistic conception of the relationship between God and the world. James never denied that it was certainly *possible* that the God experienced by human beings was also the ultimate reality in whom all things hang together in a unified way. He simply insisted that such speculation went far beyond what the evidence demanded.

Another advantage of pluralism which James noted is that it enables us to make a clear case for the analogical character of language about God. As James remarked:

> Because God is not the absolute, but is himself a part when the system is conceived pluralistically, his functions can be taken as not wholly dissimilar to those of the other smaller parts—as similar to our functions consequently. . . . Having an environment, being in time, and working out a history just like ourselves, he escapes from the foreignness from all that is human, of the static timeless perfect absolute.[19]

Classical Christian theology's use of analogy has always been plagued by equivocating tendencies, and nowhere is this more glaringly apparent than in its attempt to speak of the love of God together with his omnipotence. Like dualism but even more directly and concretely, a pluralistic conception of the relation between God and the world would spare theologians the impossible linguistic dilemmas in which they find themselves when they affirm that the living, healing historical presence in Christ is at the same time the almighty Creator of everything. On a pluralistic view, for example, the analogy between a loving person and a loving God would be sufficiently clear, even if we remained ignorant of all that being a loving God entails, to constitute an unassailable reply to Antony Flew's damning objections to the Christian use of the word "love" as applied to God.

Again like dualism, pluralism would express much better than the framework of omnipotence the living drama and force of the Christian message, with its genuine struggle between God and resistances not of his own making, its dynamic encounter between God and man in and through historical events. It would do justice to the practical religious insight expressed in the biblical apprehension of God as responding in new ways to new human situations and as deeply bound up with man's temporal existence.

Pluralism comes under the same objection as dualism from defenders of divine omnipotence: How is the victory of God assured on these terms? As in the case of dualism, this stock criticism of any view which limits God is extraordinary for the lack of thought its exponents give to the matter. All that is required is a transcendent reality among the realities that comprise "being" which is permanently enduring and "successful" in its purposes. Surely such a reality is conceivable. Once again, James would argue, it is a case of positing only what is needed for practical religious faith and hope.

The most serious objection to both dualistic and pluralistic alternatives comes from an important theme

141

in both the biblical writings and Christianity throughout its history: the conviction that God is Lord over nature as well as man and history. We have seen that the doctrine of omnipotence has been believed to be the only way to safeguard this affirmation that God creates and redeems the cosmos as a whole together with mankind. Certainly on the dualistic view there are aspects of reality which are not the creation of God, even though for the internal dualism of Brightman all reality is within the framework of the divine consciousness. For pluralism the "Lord of nature" theme is modified even more radically. As one reality among others within being, God is in no sense sovereign over, or even necessarily the ultimate context of, the universe.

There seem to me to be two possible replies, one for dualism and one for pluralism. At the outset it must be admitted, as I have pointed out earlier, that abandonment of divine omnipotence entails abandonment of creation *ex nihilo* and the classical proclamation of God's total lordship over the cosmos. On the dualistic view, Christians could still speak quite meaningfully of the lordship of God over the universe, since for "internal" dualism everything other than God exists within the divine experience; it is just that they could no longer speak of *absolute* sovereignty.

The pluralistic alternative presents more problems. Here I think that Christianity would simply have to give up speaking of God as creating, ruling, or redeeming nature and confine itself to his experienced role as healer, liberator, and fulfiller of man. On good "empirical" grounds this is entirely reasonable. After all, it is man who is religious, presumably not the rest of nature. It is man who seeks forgiveness, reconciliation, salvation, unity with the divine. In the Judaeo-Christian religious tradition in particular, man is decidedly at the forefront, and nature is often little more than the stage on which the human drama is played out. Historians of the Old Testament have long pointed out that ancient Israel first experienced God as historical liberator of man and only later came to extend his sovereignty and liberating power to nature as a whole. The linking of human creation and redemption with that of the rest of the cosmos of course reflects a profound recognition of man's participation in the natural order as a physical, chemical, biological, and psychic creature. But an inductive approach to religious experience requires only a God sufficient to fulfill human religious needs.

What man's participation in nature does suggest is that even if we speak of God only as "man's God," we must recognize that the forces which heal and judge and liberate and fulfill human beings are inextricably bound up with their existence as creatures of nature. Even on a pluralistic view there is wide scope for the activity of transcendent reality in and through nature insofar as it bears on human existence. Indeed, we may even speak of the "sovereignty" of God over human-implicated nature from this perspective—the partial plasticity not only of psychological but even of physical events in man and his environment to the influence of "suprahuman consciousness."

Modern science has given us a picture of an almost unimaginably vast universe both as to age and size, peopled to an overwhelming degree by nothing but gaseous stars and silent spaces. To consider time spans like five billion years or distances like one thousand light years would completely tax one's credulity were it not for their verifiability with scientific instruments. The great Jesuit scientist-philosopher-mystic Pierre

Teilhard de Chardin argued persuasively that the long, slow evolutionary process on the planet earth is the leading edge of the entire cosmic evolutionary process, thereby seeming to restore earth and more especially man to their pre-Copernican centrality in the universe.[20] But Teilhard himself insisted on the extreme unlikelihood of this pattern or anything like it having occurred elsewhere in the universe. While some other scientists are much more sanguine about the possibility of "intelligent life" on planets in other solar systems and galaxies, all would agree that it is probably a comparatively rare occurrence in the universe. So we have the "leading edge of the cosmic process" occurring perhaps on one infinitesimal planet, or perhaps on even one hundred or one thousand such planets, within a universe the size of which is measured in light years and the content of which is largely space and gases.

The impact of this picture of the universe upon me has been to create an intolerable strain between the idea of a God who is the ground of all reality (even in dualistic terms) and a God who actively and purposively cares about human beings. The whole thing is so out of proportion that I find it virtually impossible to hold it all together. My only surprise is that more religionists do not seem to be depressed or overwhelmed by such considerations. Of course, we have the numbers of people who have *lost* their faith in part because of their inability to feel anything but the chilliness and impersonality of the starry night's beauty. But I suspect that most believers either (a) do not ponder the world picture of science "in the guts" or quickly dismiss it when they do; or (b) take it into consideration but somehow manage to reconcile the whole thing in more or less personally satisfactory ways. In either case, I venture to say that the *real* God existentially believed in comes closer to being the pluralistic God who is not too "big" for man and his earth, who loves and purposes for us on this little planet. The Christian of case (b) may accordingly be involved in a bit of intellectual schizophrenia, not so much reconciling the cosmic God and the Savior of man as switching back and forth from one to the other. I freely admit, however, that I am perhaps incorrectly reading my own difficulties into the views of others who simply do not have such difficulties or have resolved them responsibly.

I hasten to add that there is nothing "demonstrative" about the above remarks; they are instead "impressionistic" in character. The standard rejoinder that physical magnitude is no argument against God's being both the ultimate context of the universe and the lover of man, with its usual example of the prodigious capacity of physically infinitesimal man to comprehend the universe in thought, seems to me entirely reasonable. The objection that the view I have outlined is anthropocentric, narrowly restricting God's purpose to this little planet, likewise is not without merit.

Above all, we cannot lightly dismiss the fact that a near-universal drive in developed religion is the identification of the transcendent reality man experiences as "God" with the ultimate origin, goal, and context of all reality. There is an important side of the highest forms of religious insight which seems to demand that a being fully worthy of worship or conceptually adequate to the range of man's experience and interpretation of the divine embrace the whole of reality as its matrix and destiny. This demand cannot be lightly gainsaid, and it seems to me that James dismisses it far too easily, to-

145

gether with the centuries of profound theological and philosophical reflection it has inspired.

Two things, however, need to be said at this point: The first is that if Christians want to continue to affirm the "cosmic God," they need to do so on some other basis than the doctrine of omnipotence. Some form of "internal dualism" such as I have outlined in the previous section seems to me to be the only way to envision God as the ultimate context of reality without also making him responsible for the world's evil and therefore unworthy of worship.

Secondly, I want simply to come back to my initial, admittedly personal and undemonstrative, difficulty with the tension between the world picture of modern science and the world view of Christianity. It is the tension between the powerful and mysterious, but above all humanly gracious and liberating, Presence in the life of Israel, Jesus, and mankind on the one hand; and whatever is the unimaginable, "impersonal" (the word almost inescapably forces itself out of my pen) Sufficient Reason behind a vast universe in many ways so utterly heedless of man on the other. Again, it is an impression, not an argument. But it brings home to me, in a surprisingly new way which he would not have found entirely congenial, the force of Pascal's famous phrase: "The God of Abraham, Isaac, and Jacob not the God of the philosophers."

To those Christians who share these problems, a pluralistic view such as William James suggests, or the "existentialist" alternative which we will examine in the next section, may present itself as a creative solution. For at least some believers, it may be that a "reverent agnosticism" about God's relationship to the cosmos as a whole is the only way out of a painful dilemma which does not sacrifice that "amazing grace" to man which is the indispensable heart of Christianity.

3. Existentialism

A fourth alternative is *"existentialism."* Religiously speaking, "existentialism" is the view that we should speak of God only in terms of human experience, and simply remain "reverently agnostic" about the speculative-philosophical question of his relationship to the cosmos as a whole. I have called this view "existentialism" because it emphasizes speaking of God only in terms of human existence, and because this has characteristically (although not universally or consistently) been the distinctive approach to the problem of God of the religious existentialists. The best-known example in this connection is perhaps the existentialist theology of Rudolf Bultmann.[21] Of the speculative-philosophical views pluralism is clearly the closest one to "existentialism," representing as it does an experience-rooted approach, a correspondingly man-oriented preoccupation, and an extremely cautious induction from the evidence. The two views differ, however, because "existentialism" does not want to venture philosophically beyond the God-man relationship.

Of the three alternatives we are considering, my category of "existentialism" is more nearly an ideal type than a view specifically held by certain identifiable thinkers, in contrast to dualism and pluralism. It would be virtually impossible to find a "pure" example of this perspective. What we have instead are thinkers who are decidedly "existentialist" in their approach to the problem of God, but who fail to carry through their intention with rigor and consistency. Bultmann achieves a remarkable degree of "purity" in his existentialist approach to Christianity, but as we saw in mentioning some leading twentieth-century theologians' affirmations of creation *ex nihilo,* he slips occasionally into speculative talk.

Interestingly enough, the best example of what I would call the "existentialist" perspective on the relationship between God and the world is the distinguished Roman Catholic theologian Gregory Baum, in his recent book *Man Becoming.* Father Baum, of the University of Toronto, would by no means call himself an "existentialist," but the method he follows throughout the book epitomizes what I have delineated as the fourth alternative to the doctrine of omnipotence.

Man Becoming is, quite simply, the most exciting and promising overhaul of Christian theology that has come to my attention. It should be read and reread by theologians both Catholic and Protestant, as well as by educated laypeople and the clergy. Some such reinterpretation of Christian doctrine in the light of contemporary experience as Father Baum makes seems to me to be an immensely fruitful way forward for Christianity.

Father Baum sets forth the underlying principle of his approach on several occasions, and it clearly exhibits the "existentialist" tone of his theological reconstruction: "Divine revelation is not information about God nor an explanation of the genesis of the world; rather, it is self-revelation and hence man's initiation into a new consciousness and thus a new way of being." [22] "In our theological approach," Baum states, "we reject the idea that God is an object of the intellect and that his properties can be known in a conceptual manner.

148

The knowledge of God is always salvational." [23] Here is a sharp methodological rejection of speculative-philosophical inquiry abut God and a resolutely man-centered procedure in doing theology.

Baum's method throughout *Man Becoming* is to translate all the language of Christian doctrine into statements about ordinary, secular human experience. His success in carrying out this method makes the book more nearly the fulfillment of what I believe Dietrich Bonhoeffer was beginning to work on in his last writings than anything else I have seen. Baum's method is immanentalistic but not reductionistic, "humanizing" but not simply humanistic. He believes that a fully adequate phenomenology of human experience "is able to discern transcendence in the midst of human life." [24] So, for example, while the traditional view of God as a "super-person" presiding over the universe is decisively rejected throughout *Man Becoming,* the author never reduces God to human consciousness. Divine transcendence is understood in terms of a mysterious and gracious presence to human life which is not reducible to man or his social and natural environment—which is of course the way God is encountered by man existentially.

But let us turn directly to the issue at hand. According to Baum, " 'God is creator' means that man's life is unfinished and still in the process of being created. . . . Man's development as person and as community is not a necessary evolution according to some built-in mechanism or the organic unfolding of a seed; what takes place, rather, is the repeated creation of the new, in no way derived from the elements that preceded it in time." [25] Lest the reader still labor under any ambiguity abut what Father Baum is implying about traditional creation-language, he spells it out explicitly:

149

The reader may have noticed that we have completely avoided any cosmological reference in interpreting the doctrine of God as creator. We have not said a word about God's relationship to matter, to the physical world, to the cosmos as a whole. This has been consistent with our method. For divine revelation, we have said, is not information about God nor, therefore, an explanation of the universe and its origin, but self-revelation and hence the initiation of man into a new self-consciousness. Divine revelation recreates man. If, therefore, we interpret the doctrine that God is creator, we must understand it as a declaration about human life, the faithful acknowledgment of which saves man and establishes him on the way of redemption, and not as information about a supreme, uncreated being nor an explanation of the genesis of the world.[26]

Baum considers that this thoroughly "anthropological" understanding of creation-language conforms with the biblical approach: "The Bible is almost exclusively concerned with man and his history and considers the material world only inasmuch as it contributes to man's life. The biblical accounts dealing with the cosmic order simply illustrate, announce or confirm the transformations that take place in people."[27]

Significantly, Baum goes on to say that he does not wish to preclude speculation about "the origin of the world and of matter, and . . . theories about the future development of the cosmos,"[28] even on the part of theologians. Such speculation has its importance, but "it has nothing directly to do with divine revelation and the knowledge of God. Theologians and philosophers may work out various theories regarding the evolution of the world and God's relation to this, but these theories belong purely to the intellectual order and cannot be looked upon as salvational truth."[29] This openness to the intellectual legitimacy of cosmological speculation combined with its sharp distinction from what is of concern to living faith characterizes Baum's approach to the specific issue of divine omnipotence as well.

Father Baum regards the problem of evil as "the test issue" which reveals whether a theologian "understands God's transcendence without qualifying it by his immanence and thus thinks of him as super-person above history, or whether he acknowledges a transcendent mystery immanent in the process of man's becoming and hence refuses to think of God as a supreme being over against man." [30] Baum poses the issue with admirable freshness and boldness:

> In line with our theological approach, we are unable to accept the existence of a supreme being, called God, with an omniscient mind and an omnipotent will, who has planned the world of men in all its detail and who rules over history with a power no one can resist. God is not provident, we say, in the sense that as ruler of the world he has a master plan for human history . . . by which he guides the lives of men, even while acknowledging their freedom, towards the necessary fulfillment of his will. God is not provident in the sense that he has impressed finalities on all things from the beginning so that through their interaction the world moves inevitably, even if freely, towards its destiny. We cannot accept a divine master plan in which God has permitted evil and, from the beginning, calculated its damaging effects and compensated for them in the final outcome. [31]

All this sort of traditional talk, of course, is speculative and not "salvational."

According to Baum, divine omniscience translates existentially into "the Good News that man is always summoned to greater insight, that despite the blindness and stupidity produced by sin, a mystery is at work among men as they enter into conversation and reflect

151

on their experience, a mystery that leads them into greater truth." [32] The omnipotence of God translates into the Christian experience that "there is no earthly power oppressing man that is stronger than the divine grace that frees him to wrestle with it in some way and to become more human in the process." But as "the terms are ordinarily used," Baum comments, "God is neither omniscient nor omnipotent"; [33] that is, in the traditional terms of God the supreme being presiding over the universe, of whom we have spectator-knowledge.

Specifically with respect to the problem of the relation between God and evil, we come to the heart of Baum's opposition to the traditional theological ways of speaking about our topic:

We may now say that evil is purely and simply against the divine will. There is a radical opposition between God and evil. When we conceptualized God as a supreme being ruling the world from above, it was difficult to absolve God altogether from complicity in the awful things that happen in human history. While we insisted on the biblical doctrine that there is no shadow of darkness in God, that God is love, source of life, and saviour of men, we had to admit, nonetheless, that since nothing takes place against God's will, he must at least give permission for evil. Evil, we said, is in accord with God's permissive will. [34]

Baum goes on flatly to assert that "it makes a monster out of God to suggest" that the torments and cruelties and sufferings of human life are permitted by God to happen "for a greater manifestation of his mercy in the future." "In no sense of the word," Baum concludes, "is evil permitted by him. God overcomes evil. God is constantly at work among men, summoning them and gracing them to discern the evil in human life, to

152

wrestle against it, to be converted away from it, to correct their environment, to redirect history, to transform the human community." [35]

The great advantage of the "existentialist" alternative is its intellectual modesty. It does not presume to speculate about God beyond his experienced presence and activity in human life. It keeps Christianity decisively focused where its biblical sources are, after all, for the most part focused, on the living drama of divine-human encounter. Unlike pluralism, "existentialism" at least as a general method has already established itself securely as a serious option within twentieth-century theology through the influence of existentialist philosophy, phenomenological analysis, and a new appreciation of the character of the biblical literature.

If there is a problem with "existentialism," it may be its intellectual unfinished-ness. Father Baum is substantially correct in saying that living faith does not need more than the "existentialist" perspective; that too often "spectator-knowledge" of God has seduced Christians away from the concrete demands of the transcendent presence in human life. But while he certainly allows for the legitimacy of speculative-philosophical interest in problems such as the relation between God and the cosmos, it seems to me that he drives too sharp a wedge by omitting this sort of concern altogether from "salvational knowledge." For the naturally reflective believer—not only the theologian but also many thoughtful lay persons—the search for religious truth in the wider sense of a coherent world view may be an integral aspect of his faith, his worship, and his life. I do not think we can discount the possibility that these "speculative-philosophical" concerns may have an influence on one's concrete commitments and actions. There are certain questions which human beings are driven to ask and to seek answers to, and to set them entirely to one side as "spectator-knowledge" may be not only intellectually but also existentially unsatisfying.

Nevertheless, Christian faith *and theology* would do far better to rest content with "existentialist agnosticism" if they see their only alternative as the traditional belief in the all-powerful cosmic Creator. From squarely within the Christian tradition, Father Baum has convincingly argued which of those two alternatives must be chosen by a faith which wishes to proclaim Good News and not moral and logical monstrosities.

I have discussed three "alternatives to omnipotence" in viewing the relationship between God and the cosmos. The speculative-philosophical views, dualism and pluralism, I considered to have much to commend them as both intellectually and morally responsible and as closer to living faith. "Existentialism," with its resolutely nonspeculative outlook, has already established itself within contemporary theology and offers a highly fruitful alternative, except perhaps for its somewhat arbitrary closing of the door to important questions we cannot help asking.

It is essential that theologians begin seriously considering the dualistic, pluralistic, and "existentialist" alternatives. Reverent talk about "mystery" simply will not hide the logical and moral untenability of divine omnipotence and creation *ex nihilo*. Modern Christianity's willingness to square itself with the demands of knowledge and reason has somehow—and quite arbitrarily and irrationally—stopped short at certain key doctrines and failed to follow through. There can no longer be any persuasive reason for this arrested development.

The distinctive essence of Christianity is its message of divine love, *agapē*, grace abounding in and through and beyond the ambiguities of human existence. Christian thinkers must choose between love and—not power itself, but total power. The vision of love glimpsed decisively through Christ is simply incompatible with the vision of omnipotence. One of the two must be sacrificed, and it is unthinkable to me that theologians would choose to give up that love which is the lifeblood of the faith. Even that relentless pursuer of the logic of omnipotence, John Calvin, would have denied vehemently that Christianity supremely worships naked power in its vision of deity. But there can be no other conclusion when we look at the doctrine of omnipotence squarely, unless we have decided to be so thoroughly equivocal with the word "love" as to render it vacuous when applied to God.

VI. The Logic of Ultimate Hope

Life after death has not been exactly "in" for the tough-minded, secular-oriented theologies of recent years. The more extreme forms of liberal Christian thought have even manifested a frank skepticism about the whole matter. I want to suggest, however, that faith in an ultimate purpose embracing the ultimacy of persons, however broad and attenuated in its expression, entails as part of its very logic the hope of fulfillment beyond the grave.

The logic of ultimate hope, stated succinctly, is as follows: If there is an ultimate good purpose to human life which transcends our many proximate purposes; if, further, that transcendent purpose is understood as implying the affirmation of the intrinsic value of individual human personalities or selves and their fulfillment; then it follows, in view of the personal inequities and lack of fulfillment during life on earth, that death is not the end of human existence. To put it negatively: To trust in (or even merely to hope for) a transcendent purpose involving the finality of concrete personhood, and to deny (or not to hope for) personal *post mortem* fulfillment is self-contradictory.

Now this logic does not apply on the one hand to the straightforward humanist, who wishes to combine lofty affirmation of personal human dignity with at least a practical denial of transcendent reality and purpose; such a perspective does not involve the "major" of my "syllogism." The humanist position at this point seems to me neither inconsistent nor indefensible. I would only observe, along with a number of theologians past and present and perhaps most recently by John Hick in *Christianity at the Centre,* that the full logic of a wholly secular humanism demands a finally tragic sense of life.[1] To believe passionately in the intrinsic worth of persons and in maximum personal fulfillment as the highest end of life, and yet in the face of the gross inequalities, injustices, and sufferings among men to have no recourse beyond the grave—this world view, when considered in all its starkness rather than dressed up in its usual futurist optimism, requires an admirable and stoic courage to keep from falling into cynicism and despair.

Nor on the other hand does the logic for which I am arguing apply to those religious outlooks in which individual personality is a category and a reality to be transcended. If selfhood as it is understood within the Judaeo-Christian tradition is comprehended as merely a passing phenomenon of the world of appearance and change, then clearly the "minor" premise of my argument is removed. And, in fact, we find it to be the case, consistent with this purely phenomenal concept of individual personality, that in religio-philosophical world views such as Hinduism and Buddhism the transcendent "purpose" for man involves the transcending of personal identity into the light and peace of the one infinite consciousness or of bliss ineffable. I have no wish in this essay to argue with this interpretation of human nature and destiny, which seems to be commending itself to growing numbers especially of the young in the West. I assume rather that I am chiefly addressing readers whose view of man is shaped by the distinctive Judaeo-Christian concept of the ultimacy of concrete selfhood, whether in its original theological or its more recent secularized forms.

And that is precisely my point. Even those who consider themselves extreme religious liberals generally retain, in however rarefied and qualified a form, two basic affirmations which they derive from the Christian tradition: (1) a transcendent good purpose or meaningfulness, and (2) the intrinsic value of individual human beings. For the liberal within the Christian perspective, commitment to the ultimacy of persons is so central and basic as to seem virtually like self-evident truth. He regards himself as a "humanist" in the best sense of the term—as one who is centrally concerned with man, his problems, his possibilities, his tragedies, his achievements, and whose concern usually expresses itself in active ethical form. But the liberal religionist is a special kind of humanist. He is an "ecstatic" or "self-transcending" humanist: one who trusts and/or hopes that there is a transcendent purpose which manifests itself in, and significantly embraces, human existence. No matter how broadly or vaguely this purpose is understood, no matter how tentatively and "agnostically" its affirmation is made, here is what distinguishes the humanist within a liberal Christian framework from the secular humanist.

Even the extreme Christian liberal, then, is a person

who wishes irreducibly to affirm both the "major" and the "minor" of the logic of ultimate hope. I am arguing, therefore, that unlike the straightforward humanist on the one side and some other kinds of religionist on the other, he is inconsistent if he omits or rejects the hope of life beyond death; he fails to carry through with the full logic of his perspective.

In his characteristically sound and thorough book *And the Life Everlasting*, John Baillie observed a number of years ago that in pondering the hope of life after death the question, "Do *I* want it for myself?" is not the only relevant consideration. I may believe that I have personally reconciled myself to the finality of my own death and can affirm life as meaningful without expecting more. But, Baillie went on to say, can I truly add that that is likewise all I hope for other persons—for those I love and cherish, and for victims of the many tragedies which befall human life? [2]

It seems to me that Baillie touched here upon an essential ingredient in the existential consideration of ultimate hope which is either neglected or answered in terms of tragic resignation by religious liberals who omit or reject the hope of fulfillment beyond death. To neglect it may simply reflect a failure to think through sufficiently this admittedly perplexing and obscure dimension; to resolve it in terms of tragic resignation is to take a position having no real difference from nonreligious humanism.

The exuberant affirmation of life and the world as sufficient in themselves—in which I have certainly joined along with some other celebrants of secularity—tends to be made in our society by and large by well-fed, well-educated, relatively advantaged persons. This is the characteristic milieu in which confidence in the self-sufficiency of life flourishes in affluent America—even among theologians and even after the turbulent 'sixties. As such it is the most suspect kind of this-worldliness, illustrating perhaps more graphically than any other the one-dimensionality which Baillie chided. But my criticisms in the light of the logic of ultimate hope apply also to more authentic sorts of religious world affirmation, in which the sufficiency of this life is affirmed in the teeth of personal disadvantage and tragedy.

It is often pointed out that the ancient Israelites for several centuries affirmed a robust faith in Yahweh without any belief in an afterlife worthy of hope. What must be said here is simply that they had not yet developed the full implications of their faith—in the direction either of the extent of the divine purpose or of the worth of individual persons in the light of that purpose. Significantly, too, it was partly the severe tragedies of Israel's national history beginning with the Babylonian Exile which contributed to the development of their ultimate hope. Finally, that faith which regards itself as the true fulfillment of Israel's faith centered from the beginning in the belief that Jesus' resurrection was the dramatic first installment and vindication of their ultimate hope.

On the contemporary scene there are "Christian revolutionaries," such as some of those involved in Black Power in America, the revolt of the poor here and in other countries, and similar struggles on behalf of human dignity and fulfillment, who have no use for the hope of *post mortem* fulfillment. They are usually men and women who affirm the sufficiency of this life as the disadvantaged, in the face of their own and their people's suffering and oppression. As James Cone (following Marx) points out in *Black Theology and Black Power*, the oppressor has frequently used the Christian hope of life after death as an opiate to keep oppressed peoples content with their miserable lot.[3] Among the chains which the oppressed must throw off as they seek their freedom is the pernicious and enervating doctrine that one neither can nor ought to do anything to improve his lot in life. An ideology or a theology appropriate to the revolution of the oppressed must therefore be completely this-worldly, a call to liberation and fulfillment within this life; it must react vigorously against ideas of "pie in the sky when you die" because of the way they have been used by the exploiter to keep down the exploited. "Revolutionary" theologians such as Cone accordingly emphasize the intramundane and historical dimension of the Christian hope to the exclusion of the trans-historical dimension.

One can only have the utmost sympathy with the revolutionary whose motivations and beliefs are derived essentially from the Christian perspective in his contempt for the diabolical uses to which the hope of life beyond death has been put in enslaving and keeping passive the oppressed, and in his zeal to redress the balance by proclaiming a wholly this-worldly faith. One must go on, furthermore, penitently to acknowledge the way the Christian hope of the Kingdom has been distorted in a one-sidedly otherworldly direction and used both sincerely and cynically to obstruct the humanization of man.

The fact remains, however, that the full logic of Christian hope, however liberally conceived, is profoundly dialectical—proximately historical but ultimately transhistorical, as Reinhold Niebuhr used to point out so carefully and perceptively.[4] The distinctive genius of the Judaeo-Christian perspective is that it affirms an ultimate hope which does not deny but rather embraces and fulfills this historical, concrete human existence with its hopes and achievements. Insofar as the revolutionary Christian affirms not only the intrinsic worth and dignity of individual man but also an ultimate purpose which manifests itself in, but transcends, this life, the full logic of his affirmations entails this dialectical outlook in which proximate achievements in the direction of human dignity are taken up and fulfilled in the ultimate humanization of all men beyond history.

Now at this point I would certainly be willing to argue, given the unfortunate historical and social uses of the Christian hope up to the present day, that the Christian revolutionary might legitimately refuse to talk about man's ultimate hope as a *spring for action;* although I believe with Niebuhr and others that historically the hope of the Kingdom has been able to function both consciously and unconsciously as a powerful motive and sustaining drive for creative action in the world, when it has not been distorted in a completely otherworldly direction. I can also appreciate the Christian revolutionary's reluctance even to speak of ultimate hope as a *consolation* for defeats suffered, sacrifices made, lives wasted at the hands of society, out of fear of sapping the world-directed energy of the struggle to however slight a degree; although such consolation has often functioned historically as a source of renewed courage for the struggle. It is a matter of recognizing where one's perspective leads, and perhaps in light of this being able to speak a needed word at the right time.

The religiously motivated revolutionary among the oppressed, like many of his comrades, has suffered indignities and seen others suffer to a degree which has often made him a person able to face his own death with what Heidegger would call "authenticity." That is, he may often be a person who has conquered the normal human anxiety about death to a high degree and hence is not disturbed by concerns about "ultimate consolation" or "eternal justice" as many of us are. He may live in a world where daily existence is so wretched and impoverished that one's so-called "life" is not much to lose. Insofar as it is possible to empathize as one in whose privileged social situation death is something held antiseptically at arm's length, I appreciate this attitude and deplore what has created such a despairing condition of things. But again, with whatever equanimity the Christian revolutionary views the business of death, it remains for him theologically self-contradictory to affirm a transcendent purpose embracing concrete human beings and yet to omit or deny the hope that human existence transcends death.

There is in addition, at the existential level, the possibility that the religious revolutionary who faces death and annihiliation courageously may have resolved the issue to his own satisfaction but, in Baillie's terms, have failed to think through whether this is all he hopes for others—especially for those he loves and those he has seen suffer indignities, injustices, deprivations, and untimely deaths. Furthermore, two of the most endemic dangers of the struggle of the oppressed for justice and dignity against entrenched and powerful forces are cynicism and despair. It would seem to me that the logic of ultimate hope is precisely the key to a *Christian* (rather than simply humanistic) approach to social change. A Christian perspective, however broadly conceived, is a hope-filled understanding of the struggle which transcends cynicism and despair through its trust that individual and collective sacrifices, defeats, achievements, and sufferings have not been in vain, but are taken up and fulfilled in a real and permanent way in the ultimate purpose of God. Rightly understood, this is a sustaining source of courage for the struggle which is not available to the straightforward humanist.

For the Christian revolutionary, or the Christian liberal, to resolve the issue of death in terms of tragic acceptance, then, is to take a position no different from that of nonreligious humanism on the matter. But if this is the case, then why does he want to go on talking about "ultimate purpose"? Why involve a transcendent reality such as "God," or look to Jesus more than to anyone else? Why not get "down to earth" and talk simply about proximate, finite purposes in good secular language? This seems to me to be the logical cleft stick in wanting to affirm the value and dignity of human beings *within the framework of* trust and hope in an ultimate purpose to human life, but to deny or omit life after death.

For the fact is that life is notoriously, shockingly unequal and unjust. Our own age is so keenly aware of this through social protest and the media that the point needs no laboring. The suffering and death of the young and the very young; long and pointless suffering from diseases; the appalling carnage and pain of war, which has come home to us so graphically once again in Vietnam; inexcusable oppressions and indignities and injustices suffered by countless millions of mankind; widespread poverty and lack of opportunity for a full life; congenital abnormalities, physical and psychological; crippling environmental influences. . . . The list, of course, could go on and on.

It is no accident that theodicies have traditionally relied so heavily upon the concept of life after death to rectify the injustices and render worthwhile the struggles and sufferings of this life. It is very much to the credit of a contemporary theologian like John Hick (no conservative, by the way!) to have insisted clearly and compellingly—despite his detractors—on the full logic of the Christian perspective in the light not only of the New Testament but also of the facts of life.[5]

To be sure, there is a great deal which can be said, first of all, by way of explanation of the evils in life which is consistent with an understanding of this world as an integral part of a transcendent good purpose. Secondly, there is much in human history and at the present day which is positive and creative, much in religion, the arts, ethics, human relations, everyday joys and beauty, politics, and science, which provides the religionist with grounds for his trust and hope and is seen by him as an essential and roughly coherent ingredient in a larger purpose.

It does seem to me that the evil in the world is finally incompatible with classical Christianity's belief in a God who is omnipotent or all-powerful as well as benevolent. On this view the only limitations upon God's power are self-limitations, from which I see no other reasonable conclusion than that God is ultimately responsible for evil. However, once we are willing to abandon the idea that the transcendent purpose embracing man is also the almighty Creator of the universe—a move which I maintain sacrifices nothing essential to Christianity and frees it from an impossible burden—then the compatibility of a transcendent good purpose with the evil in the world is not an insuperable problem. God is perhaps the ultimate reality behind the cosmos, but limited in his power by realities not of his own making which provide him with both opportunity and frustration. Or perhaps the transcendent reality with which Christianity believes man is in touch is not the ground of all things but one factor among many in the universe, with all the limitations that involves. In either of these alternatives, sense can be made of both the goods and the evils in human life, although not in the classical alternative of divine omnipotence.

But the incoherencies of evil remain, large and indicting. However much we may be able to "explain" them, however much we can place beside them life's goods, there remain on a purely this-worldly level the inconsolable evils of individual human lives wasted, trampled on, tortured, destroyed. To affirm an ultimate purpose involving human beings, and yet to deny or omit the logic of ultimate hope in the face of tragically unfulfilled human lives, amounts to a practical denial either that there is a genuinely ultimate purpose or that it embraces concrete personhood and its fulfillment.

I suppose someone might contend that annihilation or nonbeing at death can be seen as an eternal peace—the extinction of all the pains and injustices and tragedies which the individual has suffered. This picture of a kind of "negative Nirvana," in which all things are equalized in the everlasting rest of nonconsciousness, has a certain ostensible attractiveness about it. The main objection, however, is again that it is incompatible with any sort of real trust and hope in an ultimate purpose which embraces the ultimacy of persons. For nonbeing equals the total destruction of "person"; it can in no sense be seen as a "fulfillment" or enduring affirmation of personality in the final scheme of things. If Smith has lived a long and rich life, while Jones's life has been short and tragically deprived, it is not meaningful in any straightforward sense to say that with their mutual annihilation "everything has been made all right." There is further the basic philosophical difficulty of describing something which by definition cannot be experienced (nonbeing) as "peace," "rest," etc., since these are terms which are normally used of living, experiencing subjects. There is no "peace" if there is no one to experience peacefulness. Smith and Jones may be "equalized" in death, but of what meaning is this kind of "equality" to either of them? There is certainly no "fulfillment," but only the abrupt termination of all possibilities of fulfillment.

I suppose a word needs to be said also about the current hopes of exuberant futurists—found mainly and significantly in the United States—that science may be able on the one hand to extend our life indefinitely or to restore it, and on the other hand to create an environment with maximal opportunities for personal fulfillment and minimal inequities. Under these conditions we might imagine a person trusting in an ultimate purpose involving concrete personalities which realizes itself entirely within this life as far as those personalities are concerned. Personal fulfillment becomes possible for virtually everyone, with both environment and years on our side. One could conceive of a person, after a very long life which has afforded ample opportunity for a wide range of experiences and satisfactions, deciding finally that he is simply "tired" and submitting himself tranquilly to the annihilation of death.

The first thing to be said about this sort of hope is that there can be no excuse for *not* working to create a society and a world in which the great goods of health, at least some sort of "reasonable" longevity, and opportunity for personal fulfillment are maximized for the greatest number of persons. That is precisely what growing numbers of both religious and secular persons are rightly committing themselves to at the present time, and it seems to me to be an implication of the Christian perspective itself. But two other things need to be said by way of objection to the futurist vision as an adequate resolution of the issue of ultimate hope. The major one is simply that it solves the problem only for some perhaps distant future generation (if for them) ; it has nothing to say by way of fulfillment and rectification for the untold previous generations of human beings upon whose backs the "new world" has been slowly and painfully built. The other point to be made is simply to express a suspicion about such Utopian visions in view of the peculiar individual and social character of the human animal. From the religious perspective which derives from the Judaeo-Christian outlook, human life remains ambiguous and inequitous to the end on the plane of history. Even the "best of all possible worlds" created by man will be marked by man's flaws and characterized right up to the last trump by new possibilities for evil as well as for good. And as long as life remains only "a little bit" unjust and unfulfilling for individual persons, the logic of ultimate hope cannot be fully applied this side of the grave.

Having argued for the logic of an ultimate hope embracing but transcending history for those who still wish to affirm an ultimate purpose involving the ultimacy of persons, I am brought finally to the matter of the nature of that hope itself. Right here it is that the religious liberal often has his greatest difficulties with the whole idea, the kinds of difficulties which sometimes lead him to omit or even reject ultimate hope. I have nothing to offer here but suggestions—hints—since, although I consider the logic of the faith I have described to demand *post mortem* fulfillment, what it is remains a barely conceivable mystery.

On the basis of repeated historical examination, I happen to think there is something to Jesus' resurrection which cannot satisfactorily be explained away even on the most minimal and demythologized reading of the New Testament evidence. I say this, furthermore, from a broadly human and empirical rather than a simply theological point of view. On this level I would not want to speak of the resurrection as "supernatural" or "miraculous" in the traditional sense, but rather as an event the nonreducible reality of which suggests dimensions of human existence and experience ignored or denied under the usual canons by which empirical inquiry circumscribes itself. A variety of related phenomena in both the Christian and other religious traditions may also be found, upon rigorous examination, to possess an irreducibility which suggests the need to expand our categories of the "human," the "natural," and the "empirical." I have mentioned Jesus' resurrection because of its centrality to the Christian perspective and what seems to me to be its well-attested character.

Then there are the by no means unrelated phenomena which psychical research or parapsychology has carefully investigated over a period of about eighty years. The charlatanism which has popularly characterized the realm of the psychic should not prejudice us against the empirical possibility that there are genuine psychic phenomena. Certainly "this-worldly" psychic phenomena, such as the range of E.S.P. and "out-of-the-body" experiences, seem to be supported by a fairly impressive amount of evidence. "Otherworldly" psychic happenings such as mediumistic communication are much more difficult to deal with scientifically, and there are alternative hypotheses other than survival of death which can perhaps account for the large majority. But there remain those types, such as "cross-correspondences," as well as specific cases (in at least some of their data) which are difficult to account for on purely intra-mundane grounds such as telepathy. It is indisputable that the range of the "natural," and specifically of human consciousness, extends beyond our present knowledge. As with Jesus' resurrection, although we are here in a highly tentative and empirically complex area in which the utmost caution is necessary, some forms of psychic phenomena at least suggest the possiblity, on a strictly nontheological level, that this range may extend beyond this spatio-temporal plane of existence. To cite but one implication: While "normal" experience suggests to empirical inquiry that human personality is brain-dependent, "paranormal" experiences of the sort I have mentioned imply a more complex relationship between self and brain in which the former perhaps transcends the latter.[6]

An important function of all forms of psychic phenomena within the logic of ultimate hope is to suggest along what lines we might begin to conceive of life beyond death. For example, it has been suggested that telepathy is a model showing how communication and interpersonal relationships might function apart from sensory experience. The philosopher H. H. Price has done some careful and important "secular" analyses supporting both the empirical and the logical conceivability of the survival of personal identity beyond the death of the body, using both psychic phenomena and dream-states as models.[7]

Since the religious liberal ordinarily wants to be a good "humanist" epistemologically in his respect for, and reliance upon, publicly adjudicable and verifiable knowledge, it seems to me that the kinds of general empirical and logical considerations I have touched on will be of interest to him in helping to some small degree concretely to anchor and to conceptualize the logic of ultimate hope. But at best such data cannot take us very far in the direction demanded by faith in an ultimate purpose embracing the ultimacy of persons—as, indeed, purely general and empirical considerations cannot take us very far as grounds for faith itself. A general approach must limit itself to a purely "empirical" projection of the nature of continuance after death in terms of survival of personal identity; faith's ultimate hope looks forward to a richer, fuller reality in which personal survival and interpersonal communication are part of the larger context of ultimate purpose and fulfillment. For an open-minded historical investigation, the resurrection of Jesus is an impressive and suggestive phenomenon; for faith, it occurs within a constellation of meaning in which it helps point to an ultimate purpose embracing personal destiny.

Throughout this essay I have deliberately avoided using the terms "eternal life" and "immortality," speaking instead only of "life after death" or "*post mortem* fulfillment." The concepts "eternal life" and "immortality" are simply inconceivable. The notion of personal selves enduring endlessly, even in a qualitatively different "time," is beyond comprehension. To conjoin the notion of eternity or immortality with the affirmation of "fulfillment," as Christian thought usually does—the latter term implying as it does some sort of final or completed state—may be simply self-contradictory.

"Eternal life" and "immortality" are legitimately employed only in a highly symbolic sense to indicate that for the Christian hope human existence beyond death is a reality and a fulfillment far richer than minimal terms like "survival" and "afterlife" can suggest—a reality and a fulfillment bound up with the historic and present experience of divine and human fellowship, the presence and resurrection of Christ, and the "kingdom of God." All that is required by the logic of hope, however, is an ultimate fulfillment of human life, a fulfillment which in view of the inequities of the human situation must take place the other side of death. In what this fulfillment consists, how "long" it "lasts," are matters of which the data of faith and the more general data I have mentioned barely and tentatively scratch the surface. In the last analysis they remain largely beyond the conceptions of either belief or knowledge, and can only be hinted at by analogies from our intramundane existence.

In the last analysis the full logic of ultimate hope belongs only to the logic of faith—and it belongs there as an essential and not a dispensable or indifferent element. For faith, ultimate hope is grounded in a present trust in an ultimate good purpose for man which comprehends the intrinsic value and fulfillment of concrete persons. This trust, as I have been arguing, demands as integral to its very character this hope of life beyond death. The "five-dimensional" character of human existence, like the character of ultimate purpose itself, may be barely conceivable but is nevertheless necessary to the logic of a faith which builds, however broadly, on the central elements derived from the biblical perspective. It is certainly not necessary for Christians to spend much time in reflection on, or preoccupation with, the hope of *post mortem* fulfillment; there are too many pressing things to think about and to do here and now, and the Christian perspective calls its adherents to place them at the forefront of their attention. But that same perspective is truncated and even self-contradictory if it does not include ultimate hope. Furthermore, even for the most liberal Christian-derived outlook, that hope has a strange way of being "practical" as one addresses oneself to the issues of this life.

The apostle Paul expressed forcefully the existential upshot of a faith which tries to make sense of things without the dimension of ultimate hope: "If our hope in Christ is good for this life only, and no more, then we deserve more pity than anyone else in all the world" (I Cor. 15:19 TEV).

VII. The Resurrection: Between Scylla and Charybdis

As one who shares a considerable interest in the resurrection event, I read Antonio Gualtieri's brief article, "The Resurrection as God's Historical Deed" (*The Christian Century*, April 7, 1971), first with eagerness, then with perplexity, and finally with disappointment. Having survived the Scylla of orthodox interpretation of Jesus' resurrection, Dr. Gualtieri now seems to be sucked into the Charybdis of "existentialized" reduction of the event. Unable any longer to accept the tradition of physical resurrection and the empty tomb, he appears to believe that the only alternative is to limit the resurrection event, in a manner very reminiscent of Rudolf Bultmann, to "the release of God's reconciling and renewing power into men's lives through the death of Jesus." Like Bultmann, in overcoming the historically dubious objectivity of physical resurrection, Dr. Gualtieri has prematurely settled for an interpretation which shortchanges the genuine historical irreducibility of the Easter event. He has excluded, I believe, a middle alternative which does greater justice to the New Testament witness without driving us back to the historically problematic empty tomb stories.

What has always troubled me about existential-type reductions of Christ's resurrection into "the saving efficacy of the cross" (Bultmann) is the degree to which these interpretations read back into the New Testament documents an account of what the resurrection event "really" was to the earliest Christians which so conveniently expresses and commends itself to the perplexed modern Christian mind. Such an account seems to me to truncate the historical reality of the resurrection as it is evidenced in the New Testament.

For example, the "existentialized" interpretation of Jesus' resurrection never seems to ponder sufficiently what the very word "resurrection" meant to first-century Jews, and the corollary significance of its application to what took place after Jesus' death. In what appears to be the maximal statement of his position, Dr. Gualtieri describes the resurrection event as "the act in which God, through the obedient and sacrificial death of Jesus, was enabled to release into the world new life for those who similarly identify themselves with his way of love, the way of the cross." Now to be sure, Christ's resurrection was and is "new life" for those who existentially affirm it; it was and is, as Dr. Gualtieri says elsewhere, "God's renewing activity with power." But is this *all* the witnesses of Jesus' triumph over death meant to say by using the term "resurrection" to describe it? This is the crux of the matter. One can imagine putting it to Peter that this is what his Lord's resurrection amounts to—new divine power released into his life through all that Christ had been. "But at the bottom of all that," I think he would insist, "is the glorious fact that I saw the risen Lord!" It was a series of specific appearances at specific times and places of what was recognizably Jesus which would most naturally be described by witnesses as "resurrection" and serve as the dramatic basis of their "new life." To reduce this cause to generalized, existential-sounding terms such as "power" and "renewing activity" and put almost all the emphasis on the side of its effects in human life appears to me to be a move which commends itself very characteristically to the puzzled modern believer, but which would hardly have occurred to a first-century Jew.

Again like Bultmann, Dr. Gualtieri tends to subsume the resurrection of Jesus under the cross: "Death had not been able to stanch the flow of the sacred, renewing power that they [Jesus' followers] had known through Jesus; indeed, through his innocent and sacrificial death that power was even stronger among them." What we have here, and in similar remarks by Bultmann, is once again the reading back of an attractive modern view of the original events of Jesus' death and its reversal. This time it is assisted by taking the apostle Paul's developed "theology of the cross" as normative for the earliest Christians and by being able to draw upon many centuries of Western Christian preoccupation with cross and atonement more than with resurrection. The samples of earliest Christian preaching which we have in the Acts of the Apostles do not link Jesus' death and resurrection together in this developed way so familiar to us. As a matter of fact, in these "sermon samples" it is almost entirely the resurrection which is made the basis of the Good News. Jesus' death is enumerated among the kerygmatic events, but little is done with it theologically except to assert that it was simultaneously the will of God for his

Messiah and the cruel deed of wicked men. Here is an example from the Pentecost sermon attributed to Peter:

> When he had been given up to you, by the deliberate will and plan of God, you used heathen men to crucify and kill him. But God raised him to life again, setting him free from the pangs of death, because it could not be that death should keep him in its grip. . . .
>
> The Jesus we speak of has been raised by God, as we can all bear witness. . . . Let all Israel then accept as certain that God has made this Jesus, whom you crucified, both Lord and Messiah.
>
> (Acts 2:23-24, 32, 36 NEB)

To be sure, in the apostle Paul we have a New Testament writer who penetrates profoundly the significance of Christ's death and lays the foundations for later meditation and reflection upon the atonement. Yet Paul is at the same time precisely the one whose conversion experience is sealed by a specific resurrection appearance of Christ and whose account of the resurrection event and its meaning in I Cor. 15 is the *locus classicus* for understanding and interpreting the historical character of the event.

We do not need to bring in any material from the highly problematic resurrection narratives in the Gospels in making the case for the specifiable character of the Easter event. Paul's minimal account in I Cor. 15, with which historians generally have no quarrel, is sufficient. Here is his familiar account:

> First and foremost, I handed on to you the facts which had been imparted to me: that Christ died for our sins, in accordance with the scriptures; that he was buried; that he was raised to life on the third day, according to the scriptures; and that he appeared to Cephas, and afterwards to

177

the Twelve. Then he appeared to over five hundred of our brothers at once, most of whom are still alive, though some have died. Then he appeared to James, and afterwards to all the apostles.

In the end he appeared even to me....

(1 Cor. 15:3-8 NEB)

Paul explicitly states that he is handing on the church's early resurrection tradition (*paradosis*) which was taught to him when he became a Christian. This recorded transmission is the earliest written account of the resurrection we have. Furthermore, it is precisely the brevity and lack of elaboration in this bit of primitive tradition which also commend it to us as authentic. At least three features of Paul's account are worthy of mention.

First of all, even in this barest of resurrection narratives there is the "third day" tradition which is embellished so in the Gospels. Secondly, Jesus' resurrection is described in terms of *specific appearances* to Peter, the other disciples, and the larger circle of Jesus' followers. Paul uses only the same word "appeared" (*ōphthē*) in each case, without elaboration. Now "appeared" could encompass a variety of possibilities all the way from physical resurrection to visions. But the crucial thing is that to use *this* word, rather than some other, clearly and naturally suggests that in specific ways this Jesus who had died was somehow recognizably "seen" after his death in an exalted state.

Thirdly, Paul refers to his own "Damascus Road experience" (we do not need to depend here on the historicity of the accounts of Paul's conversion in Acts) as yet another resurrection appearance of Christ. This was important, of course, because it established Paul's credentials as an apostle or witness to the resurrection.

It is surprising to me how little is made of Paul's inclusion of his own conversion among Jesus' resurrection appearances. Here is the only eyewitness reference to the Easter event in the New Testament. Furthermore, if Paul is a witness of Jesus' resurrection, having been converted probably no earlier than five or six years after Jesus' death,[1] then this casts serious doubt on the Gospel tradition of the empty tomb and the forty-day period of appearances culminating in the ascension. If we had only the Pauline account, we would infer that the resurrection appearances lasted a somewhat indefinite period of time; that they were appearances on earth of an already exalted or "ascended" Lord; and that there was no question of an empty tomb and the glorification of a dead physical body, but rather simply of exalted appearances of one who was recognizably Jesus.

It is important to dwell a little longer on this last point, for it is central to the "middle path" which I am advocating in resurrection interpretation. Paul goes on in ch. 15, first to proclaim Christ's resurrection as the first installment of our own (vs. 20-23) and then to describe as best he can, in feeble human words, how he envisions the character of our resurrected "bodies":

The seed you sow does not come to life unless it has first died; and what you sow is not the body that shall be, but a naked grain . . .; and God clothes it with the body of his choice. . . .

It there is such a thing as an animal body, there is also a spiritual body. It is in this sense that Scripture says, "The first man, Adam, became an animate being," whereas the last Adam has become a life-giving spirit. Observe, the spiritual does not come first; the animal body comes first, and then the spiritual. . . .

179

What I mean, my brothers, is this: flesh and blood can never possess the kingdom of God, and the perishable cannot possess immortality.

(1 Cor. 15:3-8 NEB)

It is by no means unreasonable to postulate that in his speculations here the apostle Paul has in mind, and is inferring from his own experience of the risen Christ, the "first-fruits." If this is the case, then the cited passages tend to support, not the empty tomb and physical resurrection, but rather appearances of one who is just as real but who now exists in an exalted and unencumbered state—in other words, appearances of a "spiritual body." Again, if we had only Paul's resurrection account to go on I believe this would be our natural characterization of Jesus' triumph over death. (I should add parenthetically that from this point of view the stories in the Gospels of Jesus' resurrection appearances may preserve elements of authentic historical recollection, as for example aspects of the Emmaus story and the appearance of Jesus by the Lake of Galilee.)

What do we have, then, on this most minimal reading of the New Testament evidence? We have specific appearances to specific people (including an eyewitness reference) of one who is recognizably Jesus but who now exists in an exalted, nonphysical way. I believe that to explain away these appearances, in view of Paul's witness and the absolutely foundational character of Jesus' resurrection in creating the new faith which runs throughout the New Testament, as purely hallucinatory, psychologically wish-fulfilling, or fraudulent, in the manner of the secular reductionist, does not do justice to the evidence. But neither, I submit, does the theological reductionism of Dr. Gualtieri. In the light even of the most minimal New Testament evidence, to reduce the Easter event simply to "the release of God's reconciling and renewing power into men's lives through the death of Jesus" is both inadequate exegesis and unnecessary caution. It is vague where the resurrection event in Paul's account is specific; it tends to couch in quasi-impersonal terms ("power," "activity") what for the resurrection witnesses seems to have been dramatic experience of a person; it unwarrantably subsumes the resurrection under the cross; it shifts too much to the purely existential-psychological side an event to whose "objectivity" there corresponded profound existential appropriation and consequences.

It is because I am so deeply sympathetic with Dr. Gualtieri's dilemma that I have criticized the manner in which the resurrection issue seems to have polarized in his theological pilgrimage, and offered what I consider to be a more adequate middle alternative both to orthodox interpretation and to existential reduction. In rejecting physical resurrection and the empty tomb we are by no means obligated to go to the other extreme of completely "existentializing" the Easter event. The Pauline evidence affirms the specificity of Christ's resurrection as appearances without, I believe, requiring us to interpret these as the glorified resuscitation of a physical body. In fact, as I have suggested, Paul's witness points rather strongly *away* from interpreting the event in the manner of the empty tomb stories. The central point to stress here is that for the earliest Christians, the divine power and new life which they experienced existentially had their dramatic beginning and foundation in specific appearances of Jesus after his death. Nothing less would have counted as "resurrection." Nothing less, I want to suggest, would have

181

so totally turned around his followers' lives after his
death and launched them on their incredible enterprise.
While those who want to be both believers and modern
men, standing 1900 years on this side of the event, may
find a purely existential interpretation intellectually
satisfying and personally sufficient, I think it is a mis-
take to impose this view upon the first Christians.

The reductionistic mentality which is a by-product
of the success of the sciences has almost inevitably in-
fected theological reasoning. It has seduced theologians
in varying degrees into restricting transcendence to the
seemingly "safe" regions of the "inner life" and human relationships. In my own case, however, it has been
precisely my concern to be "modern," thoroughly empirical in my approach to reality, which has driven me
beyond the truncated empiricisms that dominate our
thinking into a genuinely "radical" or "integral" empiricism. A radical empiricism is truly experience-ori-
ented in being open to human experience in all its depth
and variety and surprisingness, without prematurely
forcing phenomena completely into ready-made lower
categories of explanation. This radical attentiveness to
experience has made me realize that the reductionism
which permeates our thinking is the bewitchment, the
superstition, of our intellects. It is not really "modern,"
but rather a case of arrested development, a hangover
from eighteenth- and nineteenth-century scientism. It
has been the periodic exorcising of my own reductionistic demon which has once again opened up for me the
possibility of exegeting the New Testament witness to
Jesus' resurrection without needing to "existentialize"
it entirely into the disciples' inner experience of power
and new life. The same historical evidence which makes
the physical resurrection-empty tomb tradition dubious

makes the irreducibility of specific appearances of Jesus to his followers quite probable.

Having argued for specific appearances of Jesus to his followers, I find any attempt to say what these appearances were like a matter of speculation only. Some writers, such as Joel Carmichael in *The Death of Jesus*, put the resurrection appearances in the category of "vision." [2] In his controversial book *The Other Side*, James Pike suggested that Jesus' appearances may not have been different in kind from the "communications from the dead" investigated by psychical researchers. [3] On either of these views, of course, the resurrection appearances are not unique, since there are numerous examples of visions in the history of religion and of purported communications from the dead to the living. Precisely here may lie the problem. The early Christians, who were familiar enough with reports of religious visions and probably knew something about accounts of communication from the dead, regarded Jesus' resurrection as absolutely unique in character. In any case, the most we can establish on historical grounds is the probability of specific appearances of Jesus to a large number of his followers. The nature of the appearances must remain for armchair theorizing with virtually nothing to go on from the New Testament itself.

VIII. Grace Amazing and Hell Intolerable

> Amazing grace! how sweet the sound
> That saved a wretch like me!
> I once was lost, but now am found,
> Was blind, but now I see.[1]

So run the familiar lines of John Newton's hymn,
given new familiarity in recent years by popular folk
singers. They tell, in homely and personal terms, of the
core and power and drama of the Christian message:
"amazing grace"—the astonishing, unexpected, unde-
served love of God for man decisively revealed in Christ.
Another well-known hymn echoes the "amazing" theme,
in the moving gratitude of its last stanza:

> Were the whole realm of nature mine,
> That were an offering far too small;
> Love so amazing, so divine,
> Demands my soul, my life, my all.[2]

Indeed, Christian hymnody from Aurelius Clemens
Prudentius' "Of the Father's Love Begotten"[3] to

Charles Wesley's "Love Divine, All Loves Excelling" [4]
resonates with the wonder and comfort of the divine
love which most people regard as the distinctive proclamation of Christianity. So likewise does this "agapeic
vision"—the conviction that the transcendent mystery
with which man is in touch is *agapē*: accepting, healing,
reconciling, fulfilling love—permeate Christian liturgies, prayers, devotion, mystical literature, and pious
legend. The love of God freely given to man through
Christ is the Good News which has touched and inspired and changed countless human lives throughout
the centuries.

The problem is that Christians do not really believe
that the grace or love of God is amazing. In various
ways they put limits on the divine love, qualify the
"agapeic vision": God's saving love is restricted to those
who confess Christ as Lord with both lips and lives,
or at least is partly contingent upon decisions of man's
"free will"; some human beings—perhaps a large number—are eternally excluded from the ultimate fulfillment and reconciliation which comes by divine grace,
and are doomed to an agonizing state of everlasting
alienation from God and other human beings. In other
words, God's grace is "amazing, *but* . . . ," or "amazing
for me or us, but not for 'them'." These qualifications
of the divine *agapē* have characterized Christian faith
and theology to an overwhelming degree from the New
Testament to the present. Contemporary nonconservative theology is increasingly liberated from these qualifications and sensitive to the genuinely amazing implications of the Christian message. At the same time,
however, the more usual trend among "liberalized" theologians seems to be to retain some sort of qualifications
but to interpret them in an extremely broad and open-

ended sense, and generally to avoid presuming to peer into the mysteries of salvation and rejection. Popular faith, of course, retains the old "agapeic limitations" in an often vigorous manner.

I want to argue, by contrast, that the Christian Good News of God's "amazing grace," when thought through in terms of its fullest possible implications, demands the affirmation of its universality in bringing ultimate healing, reconciliation, and fulfillment to all human beings without exception. To put it succinctly: The full logic of *agapē* entails universal salvation. My argument rests upon the following proposal: The norm of Christian thinking is the vision of the divine love, decisively disclosed through Jesus but always expanding in terms of man's grasp of its implications and never limited to its historical expressions.

Historical examination of the New Testament documents has disclosed the temporal and cultural limitations of Jesus' ministry and message. The understanding we have gained of Jesus through historical research poses the most fundamental sorts of problems for Christian theology which have not yet been taken with complete seriousness. The crux of the matter is this: Knowing what we now know about Jesus' limitation to the first-century Palestinian Jewish milieu, with the restrictions and downright errors which that included, in what sense is he any longer to be regarded as normative for Christian faith and theology?

I suggest that Jesus can no longer be normative for Christianity in the sense of looking to and justifying all his words and deeds as the standard for Christian reflection, which is still the way he is largely viewed. Theologians who have sought to take seriously and make positive use of our historical knowledge of Jesus have in various ways and degrees relaxed this traditional "christocentric" normativity, but not yet by and large consistently or very consciously. Too many still try to play the old game of bringing everything to the bar of Christ's acts and sayings, even though they are aware of the nagging possibility that historical knowledge demands a new game with new rules. The fact is that to assert with one breath that Jesus was wrong about the time of the Kingdom's consummation, about a sin which is unforgivable, evil spirits, and hell—as many nonconservative theologians freely do—and with the next breath to declare one's obedience to the Christ of the Gospels, simply does not hang together intelligibly. The standard rejoinder of contemporary theology that one must distinguish between Jesus' religious and moral authority on the one hand and, say, the errors of fact which he shared with his age (such as his believing that David wrote the psalms) on the other, will not do. The errors I have mentioned above are all *religious* (some are also factual) mistakes.

If a Christian believer or theologian starts sitting lightly to or rejecting a number of things Jesus said and sometimes things he did as well, then he has already implicitly admitted a norm other than the Christ of the New Testament himself—say the "spirit of Jesus" or "the activity of God" or the "enduring or timeless essence" which is expressed in the time- and place-bound words and deeds of the historical figure. These words and deeds accordingly need to be "interpreted," which at least in part means "liberated from their historical limitations and errors." But to have made this move—which is what virtually all nonconservative thinkers do under other names—is to have abandoned the "christocentric" norm in favor of something else.

187

This "something else" points to a much more promising and fruitful criterion for Christian understanding than what now amounts to the archaism of obedience to the Christ of the New Testament; but the new criterion needs to be consciously and clearly articulated.

The implications of historical knowledge of Jesus, then, seem to me to put an intolerable strain on the traditional view of him as the norm of Christian reflection. This strain is usually relieved in inconsistent and not-fully-conscious ways which point, however, in the direction of a norm that more nearly expresses the transcendent heart of the Christian message, is capable of endless development, and does not demand "double-think" about Jesus. I suggest that this norm is *agapē*, which finds its supreme expression in the New Testament statement that "God is love": that is, in its very being the transcendent mystery is "uncalculating, un-limited, and unconditional" caring for human beings.[5] In a word, the norm of Christian thinking is "amazing grace."

Few people would deny that God as love itself is the distinctive and powerful bedrock of the Christian message, as I pointed out at the beginning of this essay. The theme of God's "amazing grace" or *agapē* toward men shouts from virtually every page of the New Testament. It is perhaps difficult for us 2000 years later to grasp the dazzling freshness and newness with which this message must have greeted people in the first century A.D. The way in which the early Christians took over a little-used Greek word and infused it with un-precedented meaning is graphic testimony to the foun-dational character of *agapē* to the Christian perspective.

The significance of Christ for the New Testament is

precisely as the unique bearer of divine love. His words and deeds are regarded as the concrete, visible presence and activity of *agapē*, and supremely his sacrificial death on the cross. He is seen as the decisive act of "amazing grace" on the part of that God of Israel who is always "doing a new thing." Jesus is for the early Christians and for Christians down through the ages the normative revelation or disclosure of the inmost character of transcendent reality; and that character is summed up in the First Letter of John's testimony that "God is love."

Clearly, then, the New Testament and historic Christian proclamation of the love of God are completely bound up with Christ as their basis and embodiment. The question then arises: In the light of the historical problems with the normativity of Christ, how are we to understand his relationship to the "agapeic vision"? The answer does not appear to me to be difficult to arrive at: Jesus is the one through whom the "agapeic vision" of transcendence came uniquely and decisively to light in human life and consciousness. There can be absolutely no gainsaying the fact that he is the foundation of the singularly Christian conviction that "God is love"; nor should there be any desire on the part of those who must reject his normativity for Christianity to gainsay it. Herein lies Christ's uniqueness, his awesome stature among men, his continuing power to teach: He stands as the historical fountainhead of the "agapeic" perspective on the transcendent mystery.

A way into the understanding of Jesus which historical knowledge and the "agapeic" norm seem to me to demand is suggested in the New Testament iself. No matter how exalted the ascriptions bestowed upon Christ, it is clear from beginning to end that he is who he is as the emissary of God, the "Son of the Father," the supreme revealer of the divine: "My aim is not my own will, but the will of him who sent me." In other words, Jesus acquires all his meaning and significance as he who uniquely points men through himself to God, who comes as the singular representative of One who is greater than he. This New Testament recognition that Jesus is the Christ because he directs us not simply to himself but through himself to the God who is love provides a formal principle for christological reconstruction in an age when the normativity of the biblical Christ is "broken" by historical knowledge of Jesus. The historical and cultural limitations through which the "agapeic vision" initially and explosively expresses itself in the first-century Palestinian Jew Jesus point beyond themselves to a larger perspective which he unleashes but cannot contain. Indeed, the "agapeic vision" first glimpsed decisively through Christ must be seen as a norm possessing implications which unfold gradually and haltingly through the centuries, a norm the full logic of which Christians are still far from grasping, a norm which can never be identified with, or limited to, any of its particular historical expressions from Jesus to the present.

The normative question for Christian reflection, then, should not be: What does Jesus or the New Testament say? but rather: What does the logic of *agapē* suggest as we are able to grasp its implications at this point in our history? On the one hand, we have in the words and deeds of Jesus and the New Testament as a whole the many moving proclamations of the divine *agapē* as the unconditional, universal will of God for man's forgiveness, reconciliation, and ultimate fulfillment. Many aspects of Jesus' ministry, as for example his wide and profound compassion for human beings in their oppression and sickness and need, hint at the larger implications of *agapē*. In Paul's reflections on the meaning of the love of God in Christ, we likewise sometimes catch brief glimpses of a lofty and cosmic sort of the ultimate logic of "amazing grace," as when he writes of God's finally becoming "all in all"—that is, the ultimate reconciliation and fulfillment of all things in the divine love. In Jesus and the original witnesses we have, then, the presentation of the message of *agapē* with sufficient clarity to enable us to know what is contained in the idea. We also have, even in these first beginnings of the "agapeic vision" with power, fleeting suggestions of where its logic takes us. On the other hand, we have side by side with this all the talk about salvation depending upon man's free decisions as well as upon God's grace, unforgivable sins, the election of some but not all to heaven, final judgment and the separation of the "ins" from the "outs," ultimate alienation, and that hell "where the fire is not quenched." In other words, we have in the New Testament severe qualifications of the message of *agapē*.

What are the options available to Christian theology? The alternative traditionally taken, and still usually taken albeit with modifications and reservations, is to view the Christ of the New Testament as normative and to conclude therefrom that the divine love is indeed qualified or limited in the ways there stated. The other alternative, which I am recommending on the basis of the historical limitations of Jesus, is to be faithful to the implications of the "agapeic vision" as one is able to grasp them and simply to reject on this normative basis those of its historic expressions which qualify or contradict it. If the logic of the proclamation of the

unconditional, universal will of God for human re-
union and fulfillment conflicts with Jesus' sayings or
other New Testament material about hell or the contingencies of human decision, so much the worse for
the latter. The same applies to any and all historic
teachings of Christianity from the New Testament to
the present.

It should be clear from this discussion that I believe
a thorough consideration of the "agapeic vision" to demand the affirmation of universal salvation. The ultimate reconciliation and fulfillment of all human beings
are entailed by the logic of *agapē* when pondered as
fully as we are able to grasp it in the latter part of the
twentieth century.

One of the grimmest and most destructive threads in
Christian history has been the sizable majority preoccupation with final judgment and everlasting torment.
Indeed, we find almost a certain perverse fascination
with the whole matter, as when those influential theological giants Thomas Aquinas and John Calvin describe one of the delights of the blessed as the con-
templation of the tortures of the damned. Universalists
have been few and far between; one thinks of Origen
in the late second and early third centuries, John Scotus
Erigena in the ninth century, Socinus in the sixteenth
century, Friedrich Schleiermacher in the nineteenth
century, and such modern Christian groups as Universalists, Quakers, and Christian Scientists.

Happily, a small but growing number of theologians
in our time have found themselves compelled by the
logic of *agapē* to affirm the ultimate fellowship of all
men with God and one another.[6] Yet for some this
triumphant assertion of the invincibility of divine grace
still tends to be made hesitantly, quietly, or with reser-

vations. That Protestant theologian who towers over twentieth-century Christian thought, Karl Barth, provides a good example. The clear implications of his position were universal salvation. According to Barth, Christ is both electing God and elect man, and in him God's "Yes" of salvation prevails over his "No" of judgment. But because he was dominated by the need to square everything with Scripture and to preserve the freedom of God, Barth believed that he had to leave the door to hell open just a crack; after all, the New Testament contains a number of stern warnings about, and descriptions of, this state of everlasting alienation.[7] Interestingly enough, Barth's universalistic tendencies are more difficult to reconcile with the New Testament than is the traditional doctrine of hell. In drawing out such tendencies he was better than his biblicism; he was at least implicitly guided instead by the "agapeic vision" which arises out of, but cannot be limited to, the biblical events and their interpretation.

The power of Christianity's greatest "theologians of grace"—Augustine, Calvin, Jonathan Edwards, Barth— lies precisely in the ineffable grandeur and beauty of the apprehension of deity as utterly, undeservedly, unexpectedly gracious to man; "the mind boggles," as we say. All I am saying is, "Let Christians take this burning vision with absolute seriousness. Let them go on to affirm its magnificent upshot: that no human being finally can resist or stand outside the all-consuming love of God." With the equivocating exception of Barth, none of the "grace-intoxicated" theologians I have mentioned—for all their profundity of insight into what Christianity is all about—were willing to draw out the universalistic logic of *sola gratia*. All of them were dominated (for historically understandable but no

longer sufficient reasons) by the demand to justify theology at the bar of Christ and the New Testament,
which resulted in the sometimes harsh and grotesque
compromising of the "agapeic vision" by elements of
the biblical witness that severely limit or flatly contradict it. For ironically, it is precisely in such "theologians
of grace" as Augustine and Calvin that we find some of
the most religiously and morally offensive talk about
the destiny of those who are "passed over" or "repro-
bated" by God's eternal electing decree; as for example
when they speak of the damnation of infants.

At the same time, the great "theologians of grace"
must be praised for having recognized more search-
ingly than most other Christian thinkers the all-
sufficiency of divine love. In the writings of Augustine,
Calvin, Edwards, and Barth it is unmistakably clear
that "all is of God," that salvation is from beginning
to end the gracious work of God. Their idea of the
"eternal decree," based especially upon passages in the
writings of Paul, by which God has through Christ
mercifully elected or chosen human beings for everlasting fellowship and union with himself and one another completely before and apart from any merit on
their part, is the characteristic and exalted image in
terms of which they understand the absoluteness of
agapē. That for all but Barth this election is not universal, but entails the parallel damnation of many—
perhaps most—human beings, should not be allowed to
detract from the partial but powerful grasp of the
"agapeic vision" contained in the image.

But what of human freedom? Has it no role to play
at all in the issue of our ultimate destiny? Such a conclusion by no means follows intrinsically from the all-
sufficiency of "grace amazing," as virtually all the great

"theologians of grace" mistakenly seem to have thought. The "majority" position in Christian thought, with its insistence that human freedom has a role to play in our history and destiny under God, has here preserved an important dimension of Christianity's biblical roots which ought to be preserved. The problem on this side has been an *over*-emphasis on freedom at the expense of grace, just as the "theologians of grace" have under-emphasized it for the sake of grace. If an Augustine effectively eliminated "free will" in his vision of salvation, an Aquinas made salvation rest too heavily upon its contingencies. A balance needs to be struck which preserves the final all-sufficiency of divine grace demanded by the logic of *agapē* without denying human decisions a part in the particular character of the destinies which are ours both individually and corporately.

The clue to the balance seems to me to lie in the word "final." It may be that God allows a wide latitude to human freedom, and a very long time not bounded by death freely to discover ourselves and our true destiny. This would not be incompatible, I think, with the belief that at the same time he coaxes us gently along the way, "strewing our path," as it were, with "stimuli" sufficient finally to bring us to our fulfillment in fellowship with him and with one another. God may even give us enough rope to—almost but not quite—hang ourselves! Our pilgrimage to fulfillment in love may be somewhat "purgatorial" for a much longer period than our life on earth, as we painfully but richly learn through ever new experiences in which our capacity for free choice, however limited by heredity and environment, plays a unique role along with the divine grace.

The much larger aspect of this long pilgrimage which lies beyond death is of course in effect a closed book for

those of us who are still earthbound, so there is almost
no telling, from a Christian perspective, what God has
in store for man as he finds his way both gracedly and
freely to ultimate fulfillment. For Christians, Jesus'
resurrection and the embodied love it vindicates is a
decisive clue to the general character of ultimate destiny as joyous divine-human fellowship, although virtually no details are offered. At least the initial period
of man's *post mortem* existence may in part be something like what some of the more seriously regarded
claims of communication from the "dead" describe. According to these claims, the stage of existence immediately following death and evidently for some time
thereafter looks in some ways strikingly continuous
with our own, made up as it appears by the memories,
desires, and relationships "carried over" from the
intramundane sphere. Even reincarnation, an ancient
idea lately given some empirical respectability by psychical researchers, may play some role in this long
pilgrimage. But of course all these sorts of suggestions
are mere guesswork, possible hints at what lies beyond
our obstructed vision.

A vital role of freedom, together with heredity and
environment, in man's ultimate destiny would be the
unique and individual stamp it gave to each person's
pilgrimage and fulfillment. Every human being possesses a somewhat different combination of genetic and
social experience, and to the degree that he exercises
his capacity for free choice he expands that experience
in unpredictable and more intensely individual ways.
These things could be seen as furnishing the "material"
of one's own particular "working out his salvation"
both here and hereafter, since all positive views of personal survival of death agree that there must be some

sort of continuity *ante* and *post mortem* or the whole concept is without sense. On a Christian view, God's "amazing grace" would adapt its operation to the unique experience and growth of each person. The path to fulfillment in love may be especially long and obstacle-laden for some, with many wrong turnings and reroutings as a result of both genetic-environmental weight and bad choices. For others it may be shorter and more nearly a sure and steady "growth in grace."

And, of course, we need not imagine that the ultimate fulfillment of all is a kind of uniform obliteration or transcendence of all individuality and difference. The final fulfillment, like each unique pilgrimage of which it is the unique consummation, may well be imagined to be "your" destiny and "my" destiny without effacing the fact that it will also be "our" destiny and one finally determined by the divine *agapē*. Are not Christians always talking about how *agapē*-love unites God with man and man with man without destroying individual differences?

All this, obviously, is speculation, imagination—some would say pure fancy. But even though the detailed character of *post mortem* fulfillment remains finally beyond our present constricted vision, it is possible, given what seem to me to be the demands of the Christian perspective, to project in the most general terms what basic elements are involved and whether they hang together coherently. What I have tried to do is to show how it might make sense to assign an important role to human decisions even within an ultimate context of universal salvation. I have done so because I believe that both affirmations—the finality of "amazing grace" and the significance of human freedom (however restricted in scope)—are integral to the Christian perspective.

Notes

Introduction

1. Ronald Hepburn, *Christianity and Paradox* (London: Watts, 1958). See esp. ch. XI, "Scepticism and the Naturally Religious Mind," pp. 186-209.
2. Dietrich Bonhoeffer, *Letters and Papers from Prison*, ed. by Eberhard Bethge, trans. by Reginald H. Fuller, rev. by Frank Clarke *et al.* (New York: The Macmillan Co., 1967).
3. Hamilton's shift can be traced from his transitional work, *The New Essence of Christianity* (New York: Association Press, 1961), to his essays in Thomas Altizer and William Hamilton, *Radical Theology and the Death of God* (Indianapolis: Bobbs-Merrill, 1966). Like Hamilton, Paul van Buren began as a "neo-orthodox" theologian strongly influenced by Karl Barth, as can be seen in the published form of the dissertation he wrote under Barth, *Christ in Our Place* (Grand Rapids: Eerdmans Publishing Co., 1958). Van Buren is best known for his book *The Secular Meaning of the Gospel* (New York: The Macmillan Co., 1963), in which he had moved via linguistic philosophy to a kind of secular empiricism which nevertheless retained a specific connection with classical Christian theology. In the later essays which make up his *Theological Explorations* (New York: The Macmillan Co., 1968), van Buren moves even farther in a secular-empirical direction and away from an explicitly Christian orientation. Sam Keen's move from an existentialist-inspired theology to a kind of "grace-full humanism" thoroughly oriented toward psychology can be seen in his

two books *Apology for Wonder* (New York: Harper & Row, 1969) and *To a Dancing God* (New York: Harper & Row, 1970).

4. See Sartre's well-known address "Existentialism Is a Humanism" in Walter Kaufmann, ed., *Existentialism from Dostoevsky to Sartre* (New York: World Publishing Company, 1956), pp. 287-311.

5. Although these themes run throughout Camus's works, it is probably *The Plague*, trans. by Stuart Gilbert (New York: Modern Library, 1948) which presents them most fully and explicitly.

6. See Russell's much-read *Why I Am Not a Christian* (New York: Simon & Schuster, 1957).

7. See Huxley's *Religion Without Revelation* (New York: New American Library, 1957).

8. Subsequently revised and published as Woelfel, *Bonhoeffer's Theology: Classical and Revolutionary* (Nashville: Abingdon Press, 1970).

9. See, e.g., my article "Two Types of Humanism," *The Christian Century*, March 1, 1972, pp. 249-52.

Chapter 1: Christianity Beyond Christ

1. See Neil's *The Life and Teaching of Jesus* (London: Hodder & Stoughton, 1965), p. 6.

2. Schweitzer, *The Quest of the Historical Jesus*, trans. by W. Montgomery (London: A. & C. Black, 1936), p. 399.

3. *Ibid.*, p. 397.

4. Gregory Baum, *Man Becoming* (New York: Herder & Herder, 1970).

Chapter II: Albert Schweitzer on Theological Uses and Abuses of the Historical Jesus

1. See Schweitzer, *The Quest of the Historical Jesus*, trans. by W. Montgomery, 2nd ed., 4th reprint (London: A. & C. Black, 1936); two vols. which really belong together as a sequel to the *Quest, Paul and His Interpreters*, trans. by Montgomery (London: Black, 1912), and *The Mysticism of Paul the Apostle*, trans. by Montgomery (London: Black, 1931); *J. S. Bach*, trans. by Ernest Newman (London, 1911);

and *The Philosophy of Civilization,* Vol. I trans. by C. T. Campion, Vol. II by John Naish (London: Black, 1923).

2. Schweitzer's theological reflection in *The Philosophy of Civilization* is detailed and thorough; elsewhere, esp. in the primarily historical works, it is brief, fragmentary, tentative, and often unclear, as in *The Quest of the Historical Jesus.*

3. *The Philosophy of Civilization,* pp. 44-48.

4. *Ibid.,* p. 46.

5. *Ibid.,* p. 44.

6. *Ibid.,* p. 45.

7. *The Quest of the Historical Jesus,* p. 304.

8. *Ibid.,* p. 252.

9. *What Is Christianity?* trans. by Thomas Bailey Saunders (New York: Harper & Brothers, 1957), p. 16.

10. *The Mystery of the Kingdom of God,* trans. by Walter Lowrie (New York: The Macmillan Co., 1950), p. 157. *The Mystery of the Kingdom* is actually a more detailed exposition both of Schweitzer's historical approach to the Gospels and of his theological reconstruction of Christianity than *The Quest of the Historical Jesus.*

11. See *The Philosophy of Civilization,* II, 94-102.

12. *Ibid.,* I, 68-69.

13. *Ibid.,* 86.

14. *Out of My Life and Thought,* trans. by C. T. Campion (New York: New American Library, 1953), p. 45.

15. *The Mystery of the Kingdom,* p. 158.

16. *Ibid.,* pp. 158-59; italics mine. See also *The Mysticism of Paul the Apostle,* p. ix: "The investigation of historical truth in itself I regard as the ideal for which scientific theology has to strive."

17. *The Mystery of the Kingdom,* p. 158; italics mine.

18. *The Quest of the Historical Jesus,* p. 399; italics mine.

19. *Ibid.,* p. 398. See also p. 397: "Although historical knowledge can no doubt introduce greater clearness into an existing spiritual life, it cannot call spiritual life into existence."

20. *The Mysticism of Paul the Apostle,* p. 395.

21. *Out of My Life and Thought,* p. 46.

22. *Ibid.,* p. 46.

23. *The Quest of the Historical Jesus,* pp. 399-400; italics mine.

24. *Ibid.,* p. 400.

25. *Out of My Life and Thought,* p. 47.

26. *Ibid.,* p. 48.

27. *The Mysticism of Paul the Apostle,* p. ix.

28. Among Bultmann's representative works are *The History of the Synoptic Tradition,* trans. by John Marsh (New York:

Harper & Row, 1963); *Jesus and the Word*, trans. by Louise
Pettibone Smith and Erminie Huntress Lantero (New York:
Charles Scribner's Sons, 1958); *Primitive Christianity*, trans.
by R. H. Fuller (New York: Meridian, 1956); *Theology of
the New Testament*, 2 vols., trans. by Kendrick Grobel (New
York: Charles Scribner's Sons, 1951, 1955); "Jesus Christ
and Mythology," in Hans W. Bartsch, ed., *Kerygma and
Myth*, Vol. I, trans. by R. H. Fuller (New York: Harper
& Brothers, 1961), pp. 1-44; and *Jesus Christ and Mythology*
(New York: Charles Scribner's Sons, 1958).
29. *The Quest of the Historical Jesus*, p. 397.

Chapter III: Creation ex nihilo: Paradox or Contradiction?

1. *The Shorter Oxford English Dictionary*, third ed., rev. and
ed. by C. T. Onions (London: Oxford University Press, 1964),
p. 1428; italics mine.
2. *Ibid.*, p. 1835.
3. Langdon Gilkey, *Maker of Heaven and Earth* (Garden City,
N. Y.: Doubleday & Co, 1959), p. 46.
4. *Summa Contra Gentiles* II, 16, in Thomas Aquinas, *Theological Texts*, selected and trans. with notes and intro. by
Thomas Gilby (London: Oxford University Press, 1955), p.
77.
5. Disputations, *de Potentia* III, 15, in Gilby, p. 82.
6. Emil Brunner, *The Christian Doctrine of Creation and Redemption*, trans. by Olive Wyon (Philadelphia: The Westminster Press, 1952), p. 9.
7. *Ibid.*, p. 11.
8. *Ibid.*, p. 12; italics mine.
9. Paul Tillich, *Systematic Theology*, I (Chicago: University of
Chicago Press, 1951), 253.
10. *Ibid.*, pp. 253-54.
11. *Ibid.*, p. 253.
12. Gilkey, *Maker of Heaven and Earth*, p. 53.
13. *Ibid.*, p. 65.
14. Ian Barbour, *Issues in Science and Religion* (New York:
Harper & Row, 1971), p. 383.
15. *Ibid.*, p. 384. The reference is to Jaroslav Pelikan, "Creation
and Causality in the History of Christian Thought," in Sol
Tax, ed., *Evolution After Darwin*, 3 vols. (Chicago: University of Chicago Press, 1964), Vol. 3.

16. *Ibid.*, p. 458; italics mine.
17. See Brightman's *A Philosophy of Religion* (Englewood Cliffs, N. J.: Prentice-Hall, 1940), pp. 315-18, 331-34.
18. Barbour, *Issues in Science and Religion*, pp. 444, 457.
19. *The Interpreter's One-Volume Commentary on the Bible*, ed. by Charles M. Laymon (Nashville: Abingdon Press, 1971), p. 3.
20. *Timaeus*, trans. by Francis M. Cornford (Indianapolis: Bobbs-Merrill, 1959), p. 19.
21. Brightman, *A Philosophy of Religion*, pp. 331-34, 336-40.
22. *Ibid.*, p. 314.
23. See, e.g., the discussion in Arend Th. van Leeuwen, *Christianity in World History*, trans. by H. H. Hoskins (London: Edinburgh House Press, 1964), pp. 63-67.
24. *The Interpreter's One-Volume Commentary on the Bible*, p. 4.
25. See, e.g., Gregory Baum, *Man Becoming;* esp. ch. VII, "Divine Creation."

Chapter IV:
The Dilemma of Omnipotent Love

1. Antony Flew and Alasdair MacIntyre, eds., *New Essays in Philosophical Theology* (New York: The Macmillan Co., 1955), pp. 96-108.
2. *Ibid.*, pp. 97-98.
3. *Ibid.*, p. 98.
4. *Ibid.*, p. 97.
5. *Ibid.*, p. 99.
6. Camus, *The Plague*, pp. 196-97.
7. Flew, *New Essays*, pp. 104-5.
8. *Ibid.*, p. 105.
9. *Ibid.*, p. 107.
10. Ibid., p. 164.
11. *Ibid.*, p. 168.
12. *Ibid.*, p. 165.
13. John Hick, *Philosophy of Religion* (Englewood Cliffs, N. J.: Prentice-Hall, 1963), p. 38.
14. See, e.g., Joseph Fletcher, *Situation Ethics* (Philadelphia: The Westminster Press, 1966), p. 97.
15. See Lewis' *Mere Christianity* (London: Collins, 1955), esp. pp. 42-48. In his book *God and Philosophy* (London: Hutchinson & Co., 1966), skeptic Antony Flew insists upon doing battle primarily with traditional (not even post-Vatican II!)

Roman Catholic orthodoxy; see, e.g., pp. 16-19. Eminent skeptics like Ludwig Feuerbach and Sigmund Freud are known for their contempt of "liberalizing" tendencies in religion and their insistence upon rejecting it at its most orthodox, not to say its most popular and primitive; see, e.g., Feuerbach's *The Essence of Christianity*, trans. by George Eliot (New York: Harper & Brothers, 1957), and Freud's *The Future of an Illusion*, trans. by W. D. Robson-Scott, rev. and newly ed. by James Strachey (Garden City, N. Y.: Doubleday & Co., 1961).

16. Karl Barth, *Dogmatics in Outline*, trans. by G. T. Thomson (New York: Harper & Brothers, 1959), p. 49.

17. *Ibid.*, pp. 46-47.

18. Emil Brunner, *The Christian Doctrine of God*, trans. by Olive Wyon (Philadelphia: The Westminster Press, 1950), p. 250.

19. *Ibid.*, p. 251.

20. *Ibid.*, p. 250.

21. Rudolf Bultmann, *Existence and Faith*, selected, trans., and intro. by Schubert M. Ogden (New York: Meridian Books, 1960), p. 175.

22. *A New Catechism*, trans. by Kevin Smyth (New York: Herder & Herder, 1967), pp. 492-93.

23. See, e.g., Hick's *Christianity at the Centre* (London: SCM Press, 1968), esp. pp. 8-16.

24. Hick, *Philosophy of Religion*, p. 40.

25. *Ibid.*, pp. 40-41.

26. Brightman, *A Philosophy of Religion*, p. 314; italics mine.

27. Hick, *Philosophy of Religion*, p. 44.

28. *Ibid.*, pp. 45-46.

29. Hick, *Christianity at the Centre*, pp. 90-91.

30. *Ibid.*, pp. 91-92.

31. *Ibid.*, p. 92.

Chapter V:
Alternatives to Omnipotence

1. Brightman, *A Philosophy of Religion*, p. 313.

2. *Timaeus*, pp. 19-21.

3. Brightman, *A Philosophy of Religion*, esp. pp. 319-21.

4. *Ibid.*, pp. 336-37.

5. *Ibid.*, p. 337.

6. *Ibid.*, p. 338.

7. *Ibid.*, pp. 331-32.

8. *Ibid.*, p. 333.
9. *Ibid.*, p. 334.
10. *Ibid.*, p. 316.
11. *Ibid.*, p. 317.
12. *Ibid.*, p. 318.
13. *Ibid.*, p. 328.
14. C. S. Lewis, *Mere Christianity*, (London: Collins, 1955), p. 47.
15. Brightman, *A Philosophy of Religion*, p. 331.
16. William James, *The Varieties of Religious Experience* (New York: New American Library, 1958), p. 395.
17. *Ibid.*, p. 396.
18. James in *Essays in Radical Empiricism* and *A Pluralistic Universe*, ed. by Ralph Barton Perry (New York: E. P. Dutton, 1971), p. 269.
19. *Ibid.*, p. 272.
20. See, e.g., Teilhard's essays in *The Future of Man* (New York: Harper & Row, 1964).
21. See esp. Bultmann's "New Testament and Mythology," in Hans W. Bartsch, ed., *Kergyma and Myth*, I, trans. by R. H. Fuller (New York: Harper & Brothers, 1961), 1-44; and *Jesus Christ and Mythology* (New York: Charles Scribner's Sons, 1958).
22. Baum, *Man Becoming*, p. 246.
23. *Ibid.*, p. 237.
24. *Ibid.*, p. xiv.
25. *Ibid.*, p. 216.
26. *Ibid.*, p. 218.
27. *Ibid.*, p. 219.
28. *Ibid.*, p. 220.
29. *Ibid.*, pp. 220-21.
30. *Ibid.*, pp. 241-42.
31. *Ibid.*, p. 242.
32. *Ibid.*, p. 243.
33. *Ibid.*, p. 244.
34. *Ibid.*, pp. 244-45.
35. *Ibid.*, p. 245.

Chapter VI:
The Logic of Ultimate Hope

1. Hick, *Christianity at the Centre*, pp. 13-16.
2. John Baillie, *And the Life Everlasting* (London: Epworth Press, 1961), pp. 40-47.

3. James Cone, *Black Theology and Black Power* (New York: The Seabury Press, 1969), pp. 121-27.
4. See, e.g., Niebuhr's *Faith and History* (New York: Charles Scribner's Sons, 1949), ch. XIII, "Fulfillments in History and the Fulfillment of History," pp. 214-34.
5. See Hick's *Christianity at the Centre*, pp. 82-92.
6. Among the many books on psychical research, mention should be made of the following reputable works: Gardner Murphy, *The Challenge of Psychical Research* (New York: Harper & Row, 1961); C. D. Broad, *Lectures on Psychical Research* (London: Routledge & Kegan Paul, 1962); and H. Richard Neff, *Psychic Phenomena and Religion* (Philadelphia: The Westminster Press, 1971).
7. See H. H. Price, "Personal Survival and the Idea of Another World," in John Hick, ed., *Classical and Contemporary Readings in the Philosophy of Religion* (Englewood Cliffs, N. J.: Prentice-Hall, 1964), pp. 364-86.

Chapter VII: The Resurrection: Between Scylla and Charybdis

1. See John Knox, *Chapters in a Life of Paul* (Nashville: Abingdon Press, 1950), pp. 65, 74-88.
2. Joel Carmichael, *The Death of Jesus* (New York: Dell Books, 1962), pp. 167-84.
3. James Pike, *The Other Side* (New York: Dell Books, 1968), pp. 240-49.

Chapter VIII: Grace Amazing and Hell Intolerable

1. "Amazing Grace," as it appears in *The Methodist Hymnal* (Nashville: The Methodist Publishing House, 1964), no. 92.
2. "When I Survey the Wondrous Cross," *Ibid.*, no. 435.
3. *Ibid.*, no. 357.
4. *Ibid.*, no. 283.
5. The adjectives are from Anders Nygren's classic study *Agape and Eros*, trans. by Philip S. Watson (Philadelphia: The Westminster Press, 1953), p. 91. Nygren's method, by which he isolates *agapē* as the "fundamental motif" of Christianity, is very pertinent to what I am proposing, as well as a

thorough examination of the treatment of *agapē* throughout the history of Christian thought.

6. See, e.g., Paul Tillich, *Systematic Theology*, III (Chicago: University of Chicago Press, 1963), 406-23; Emil Brunner, *The Christian Doctrine of the Church, Faith, and the Consummation*, trans. by David Cairns (Philadelphia: The Westminster Press, 1962), ch. 10, "Universalism and World Judgment," pp. 415-24; John Hick, *Christianity at the Centre*, pp. 90-92, 99-117.

7. For a succinct and accurate discussion of Barth's sprawling discussion of election, see Herbert Hartwell, *The Theology of Karl Barth: An Introduction* (Philadelphia: The Westminster Press, 1964), pp. 105-12.